Eating Clean Vegetarian Cookbook

EATING CLEAN

Vegetarian Cookbook

85 Easy, Plant-Based Recipes
to Help You Feel Your Best

KATHY SIEGEL, MS, RDN, CDN

ROCKRIDGE
PRESS

For general information on our other products and services or to obtain technical support, please contact our Customer Care Department within the United States at (866) 744-2665, or outside the United States at (510) 253-0500.

Rockridge Press publishes its books in a variety of electronic and print formats. Some content that appears in print may not be available in electronic books, and vice versa.

Interior and Cover Designer: Monica Cheng
Art Producer: Hannah Dickerson
Editor: Kelly Koester
Production Manager: Jose Olivera
Production Editor: Melissa Edeburn

Photography © 2021 Andrew Purcell; food styling by Carrie Purcell.

ISBN: Print 978-1-64876-500-1 | eBook 978-1-64739-588-9
R0

CONTENTS

INTRODUCTION

What exactly is eating clean?

There are many approaches, but most experts agree that eating clean is about incorporating more whole foods into your diet in their most natural state, while avoiding processed foods as much as possible. That can be hard to do when you're following a vegetarian life-style because so many vegetarian foods are actually highly processed. But the health benefits of both a plant-based diet and eating clean are numerous and well documented (more about that in chapter 1), making it well worth the effort.

I know what you're thinking: Will eating clean really make me feel good? Do I have to give up delicious food? Will vegetarian dishes truly satisfy me? I've heard all of your concerns, and I am here to assure you that you will not only enjoy the healthy, plant-based recipes in this book but also continue to enjoy

foods you crave while feeling satisfied and great.

I understand the many challenges of adopting this kind of lifestyle. I, too, want to feed myself and my family clean, nutrient-dense foods, but many days I run short on time. My family and I want to enjoy comforting, familiar foods as well, but often those dishes are not rich in nutrient-dense ingredients. I want to entertain my friends, but I worry they won't find my plant-based dishes enjoyable and satisfying.

As a nutritionist, mother, and advocate for plant-based eating, I am passionate about helping others eat healthy at every meal. I have faced the same challenges you have. Being too busy is a perfect excuse to pick up take-out and avoid cooking more nutritious food. But eating healthy, plant-based meals does not have to be a struggle. In fact, it's easy to prepare clean, vegetarian meals and snacks when you have a well-stocked kitchen, and they will taste incredible with the right seasonings. So, in addition to 85 recipes, I'll give you a list of ingredients to have on hand so you can quickly create dishes that will nourish you in every way.

I have made it my focus to create more plant-based, nutrient-dense dishes that taste delicious. It's actually not difficult. The reality is, most nutrient-dense vegetarian foods, such as fruits, vegetables, whole grains, legumes, nuts, and seeds, have delicious flavor all on their own, and when you combine them with herbs and spices, you can create the most flavorful, fresh dishes. Plus, all of these foods are packed with nutrients and fiber to satisfy you and make you feel great.

I want you to love what you eat. My hope is that this cookbook will inspire you to truly enjoy eating cleaner, more nutrient-dense, plant-based foods. The recipes here will make your meals exciting and delicious, as well as make you feel great! I am thrilled to be on this journey to better eating with you.

CHAPTER 1

WELCOME TO EATING CLEAN AND VEGETARIAN

Is it possible to eat clean and vegetarian without sacrificing delicious, filling food? It's possible! In the second part of this book, I'll be sharing with you delicious plant-based, whole-food recipes that will satisfy you and your entire family. But first I want to talk about what clean eating is and why it's so good for you and your family. And I'll give you some very specific advice on how to set up your kitchen for success.

A Brief Introduction to Eating Clean and Vegetarian

Eating clean means enjoying more plant-based whole foods and limiting your consumption of heavily processed foods. Essentially, it's eating foods in their more natural state—minimally processed and unrefined.

It also means nourishing your body with foods such as fruits and vegetables, whole grains, beans, legumes, nuts and seeds, and healthy fats. When you choose whole foods—nutrient-dense and closest to their natural state—you will be eating foods that are naturally higher in fiber, vitamins, and minerals.

A vegetarian diet is not always clean, though. The biggest misconception about vegetarian dishes is that if they're meatless, they must be healthy. Vegetarian dishes may focus on plant-based ingredients, but they can also include heavily processed foods. Read the nutrition labels and you will find packaged vegetarian foods that are high in refined sugar, sodium, unhealthy fats, artificial sweeteners and colors, and preservatives. When you stay away from processed foods and stick with whole foods in as close to their natural state as possible, you avoid these ingredients.

Eating clean and vegetarian can be a natural fit, though, combining more nutrient-dense, whole foods with fewer animal proteins to provide the necessary nutrients for your good health. I am here to show you how to combine the two concepts to create a healthy lifestyle, with plant-based recipes and tips that will have you feeling great! Let's start with the principles of clean eating, so you can best understand how to get started.

The Principles of Eating Clean

Understanding clean eating starts with some principles about the high-quality, nutrient-dense foods you should be adding to your meals and snacks in a more balanced way, and the heavily processed foods and additives you should be avoiding. I am excited to introduce you to this plan!

EAT WHOLE FOODS

Your eating-clean vegetarian lifestyle should include mostly whole foods. Whole foods are nutrient-dense foods that are closest to their natural state—unprocessed or minimally processed, and unrefined. Whole foods include fruits and vegetables, whole grains, nuts, seeds, pulses, and legumes, and may also include some high-quality animal proteins such as dairy products and eggs. Eating more whole foods will create a diet that is naturally high in the nutrients necessary for your optimal health.

AVOID PROCESSED, REFINED, AND PACKAGED FOODS

Avoid (or at least limit) these kinds of foods when you're following an eating-clean plan. Processed food is any food that is altered from its natural state. There are varying degrees of food processing: It can be as simple as food being cooked, canned, or frozen (minimally processed), or can be more drastic when food is altered nutritionally and its original ingredients are barely recognizable (heavily processed). Minimally processed foods may still retain their nutrients and fit well in an eating-clean diet. However, heavily processed foods are typically the items with long lists of ingredients that reveal high amounts of sodium, refined sugar, unhealthy fats, artificial sweeteners and colors, as well as preservatives and other chemicals. These foods typically have low nutritional quality and high energy density (the number of calories per portion).

BALANCE YOUR PLATE

Well-balanced meals and snacks are important parts of an eating-clean lifestyle. To better understand what a balanced plate is, imagine a plate that's divided into quarters. Half of your plate should be filled with fiber-rich fruits and vegetables, one-quarter should be protein-rich foods, and one-quarter should include complex carbohydrates. Put a little circle of healthy fats right in the center. I'll discuss how to build your balanced plate in more detail later in this chapter, but it's helpful to visualize your balanced plate when you're putting together a meal.

WATCH YOUR SALT INTAKE

Many Americans consume way more sodium than is healthy; typically, it comes from heavily processed foods. Too much sodium in your diet has been associated with an increased risk of high blood pressure and heart disease. Aiming for less than 2,300 mg of sodium per day for adults will help you achieve a healthy eating pattern, according to the 2020–2025 Dietary Guidelines for Americans. I've limited the added salt in the recipes in this book to encourage a healthy daily amount. In the short term, your taste buds may notice the difference, but in the long term, foods you once thought were just right will eventually taste too salty, and the natural flavors of whole foods will shine through.

FOCUS ON HEALTHY FATS

The quality of the fat you include in your meals and snacks is an important part of better health. It's not necessary to avoid all fat—in fact, healthy fats are critical for proper nutrition. But there are two main types of fat you need to avoid or limit while following an eating-clean plan: saturated fats and trans fats. Saturated fats are primarily found in red meat, poultry, coconut oil, and full-fat dairy. Trans fats are found primarily in heavily processed foods and are formed as a result of a process called partial hydrogenation, in which hydrogen is added to vegetable oil to increase its shelf life. Both of these fats may raise your LDL (bad) cholesterol levels and increase your risk of developing cardiovascular disease. Incorporating monounsaturated fats and polyunsaturated fats as whole foods, including olives, avocados, nuts, and seeds, can help promote good health and raise your HDL (good) cholesterol. Healthy oils, such as extra-virgin olive oil and avocado oil, are processed, because they are extracted from the whole food, but the processing is minimal, and when used in moderation, they can be beneficial.

REDUCE YOUR SUGAR CONSUMPTION

Reducing the amount of sugar you consume is important to better control your weight and reduce your risk of developing chronic health problems such as diabetes and heart disease. Some high-sugar foods to avoid, such as packaged cookies and cakes, are obvious. However, sugar is hidden in many less obvious processed foods, even some savory ones. Condiments such as ketchup, mustard, tomato sauce, and salad dressing may contain high amounts of sugar. Other less obvious foods such as yogurt, nut butters, dairy-free milks, and bread can be packed with refined sugar, too. Before you add any processed food to your shopping cart, always read the label.

EXERCISE REGULARLY

Incorporating daily movement is also an important part of the eating-clean vegetarian lifestyle. Did you know that regular exercise may help you maintain a healthy digestive system? And proper digestion leads to better absorption of nutrients. Exercise can vary from gentle and restorative to strenuous. Depending on your situation and overall health, strenuous exercise could actually add stress that may negatively affect digestion, but more restorative to moderate exercise can be beneficial to incorporate daily. This kind of exercise includes walking, stretching, gentle weight-bearing exercises, yoga, and even daily chores.

Eating Clean vs. Cleanses and Detoxes

Let me start off by saying I am all for ridding your body of harmful chemicals and toxins, but by feeding yourself clean foods, not by starving yourself of important nutrients. Many cleanses and detoxes advertise that they eliminate toxins from your body, but they mostly restrict important nutrients, such as protein, fiber, fatty acids, vitamins, and minerals, by eliminating them entirely.

It's true that when toxins build up, your health can suffer, so it's important to feed your body consistently and well to eliminate this cycle. When you eat clean, nutrient-dense foods, your body can easily get rid of harmful toxins without quick-fix diets or intense detoxes. Your body is capable of naturally cleansing and detoxing through the liver, colon, kidneys, and skin, and you can support it by feeding it nourishing foods.

Clean eating is a lifestyle, not a quick fix; it's a way of feeding your body to feel good every day. So instead of starving your body, nourish it with plant-based whole foods that are nutrient-dense to allow your body to heal and cleanse itself naturally.

What It Means to Be a Vegetarian

Being a vegetarian simply means eating no meat (beef, pork, lamb, and game), poultry (chicken, turkey, duck, and other fowl), fish and shellfish, insects, animal stocks and fats, and animal byproducts such as rennet (used in making certain cheeses) and gelatin. However, many vegetarians do eat byproducts of animals that did not involve slaughtering the animal. Those byproducts might include eggs, dairy products, and honey. Let's take a closer look at the various types of vegetarians.

Lacto-ovo-vegetarians avoid all types of meat, poultry, and fish but do eat dairy products and eggs.

Lacto-vegetarians avoid meat, poultry, fish, and eggs but do eat dairy products.

Ovo-vegetarians avoid meat, poultry, fish, and dairy products but do eat eggs.

Vegans avoid all products that come from animals—even honey.

This cookbook will focus on the lifestyle of lacto-ovo-vegetarians. Therefore, some recipes include eggs, dairy products, or honey, but all exclude meat, poultry, seafood, gelatin, and animal rennet, as well as stock and fat from animals. You will also find quite a few vegan recipes here.

The Health Benefits of Eating Clean and Vegetarian

Researchers believe that eating a diet rich in fiber, antioxidants, vitamins, minerals, phytonutrients, and healthy unsaturated fats (such as in a vegetarian whole-food diet) promotes an anti-inflammatory response in the body that may reduce the risk of developing many chronic diseases. The 2020–2025 Dietary Guidelines for Americans emphasizes eating more nutrient-dense foods, including whole grains, fruits, vegetables, beans, nuts and seeds, and less animal protein for better nutrition and health across a person's life span. Here are a few health benefits you may experience when living an eating-clean vegetarian lifestyle.

INCREASED ENERGY LEVELS

The types of foods you eat affect your energy levels. Choosing a varied diet of nutrient-dense foods and avoiding foods high in sugar and saturated and trans fats will provide you with the necessary nutrients to increase your energy level and help you maintain alertness. The fiber found in these nutrient-dense foods is digested more slowly as well, leaving you with a steady supply of energy.

IMPROVED DIGESTION

A diet rich in nutrient-dense, fiber-rich foods and low in heavily processed foods is best for optimal digestion. Fiber helps regulate digestion and head off problems by adding bulk to your stool and therefore reducing constipation. Research also has shown that fiber-rich foods (such as a variety of fruits, vegetables, beans, legumes, and whole grains) may help with gut health. Some fibers even act as prebiotics to help feed the healthy bacteria in your gut, which aids in digestion and helps lower inflammation throughout the body.

BETTER SLEEP

Studies have shown that eating more fiber-rich foods is associated with more restorative sleep. Soluble fiber, found in foods such as oats, black beans, avocados, and flaxseed, can slow the absorption of sugar and help prevent spikes in blood sugar that may lower the body's levels of melatonin, a hormone that regulates the sleep-wake cycle and is important for better sleep. In addition, consuming magnesium-rich foods, such as nuts, seeds, leafy greens, whole grains, dairy, and beans, can help relieve anxiety and calm you so you can get a good night's rest.

STRONGER IMMUNE SYSTEM

When a diet lacks important nutrients, including vitamins and minerals, you may compromise your immune function and increase your risk of infection. Vitamin C (found in fruits and vegetables) may increase your production of white blood cells—important for a healthy immune system. Zinc and selenium (minerals found in nuts and seeds) are essential for a well-functioning immune system as well. Deficiencies in either can increase your susceptibility to infection, as well as make recovery more difficult. And vitamin D (found in eggs, dairy, and mushrooms—the only plant-based sources) supports healthy lungs and immune health, and helps regulate inflammation in the body. Consuming a variety of antioxidant-rich foods, such as fruits, vegetables, legumes, and whole grains, will naturally help your immune system fight against organisms that cause infections.

DECREASED RISK OF HEART DISEASE, DIABETES, AND CANCER

Recent studies, including a 2019 study published in the *British Medical Journal*, found that individuals who eat fewer heavily processed foods are at a lower risk of developing cardiovascular, coronary, and cerebrovascular diseases. Those who eat a diet high in fiber-rich foods may also reduce their risk of developing heart disease, obesity, and type 2 diabetes, according to two large studies of American men and women. Finally, the American Institute of Cancer Research suggests that a vegetarian diet may significantly reduce the risk of developing certain cancers, including stomach, colon, breast, and ovarian cancers.

The Clean, Balanced Vegetarian Plate

Earlier I explained that on a balanced plate, at least half, the greatest portion, should be filled with a variety of fiber-rich vegetables and fruits. Vegetables and fruits are packed with phytonutrients, antioxidants, vitamins, and minerals—important nutrients to promote optimal health. Choose a variety of colors of fruits and vegetables to best meet your nutritional needs; those different colors tell you that different nutrients can be found in the produce. Organic produce is best, but if it's unavailable or not within your budget, it's always better to eat more fruits and vegetables, regardless of whether they're organic.

One-quarter of your balanced plate should be protein-rich foods: plant-based proteins, dairy, and eggs. Plant-based proteins—which include lentils, beans, seitan (made from gluten, the main protein in wheat), soybeans, chickpeas, nuts, and seeds—provide important vitamins, minerals, antioxidants, healthy fats, and fiber. Tofu and tempeh are derived from soybeans and are an excellent source of

plant-based protein. However, the controversy around the potential risks of consuming genetically modified (GMO) soy means it's best to choose organic, less-processed soy products.

Dairy and eggs are also part of the eating-clean vegetarian lifestyle. When you buy dairy products, be sure to read the labels carefully to avoid brands with fillers and added sugars. When possible, avoid dairy produced from cows treated with the growth hormones rBGH and BGH or with antibiotics. These additives are never used in organic dairy products, but if organic isn't in your budget, check the labels for these additives and try to avoid them.

As far as eggs go, when possible, purchase eggs from pasture-raised hens. Pasture-raised eggs have been shown to have greater nutritional value, with higher levels of omega-3 fatty acids and vitamin E. They also come from hens who have spent their entire lives outdoors, enjoying a more natural diet of plants, insects, and grains.

The other quarter of your clean, balanced vegetarian plate should be filled with complex carbohydrates. Although there are a lot of fad diets that require you to eliminate carbs entirely, complex carbohydrates are an important source of energy for your body and should always be included on your balanced plate. Complex carbs include whole grains such as brown rice, sorghum, freekeh, millet, oats, and quinoa, as well as beans, lentils, chickpeas, and potatoes. These kinds of carbohydrates keep you feeling full, as they are fiber-rich and take more time for your body to digest. Minimally processed products such as legume and lentil pasta, 100 percent whole-grain bread, and brown rice noodles are great complex carbs to enjoy as well.

Healthy fats should be added to your plate in the smallest portions. Whole-food plant-based fat choices include olives, avocados, nuts, and seeds. Extra-virgin olive oil and avocado oil should be added more sparingly. Always try to limit or avoid saturated fats and trans fats.

Finally, remember to drink plenty of water! Water is essential for every cell, tissue, and organ in your body to function at its best.

10 Amazing Sources of Vegetarian Protein

You may wonder if it's possible to eat enough protein on a vegetarian diet, but the good news is that enjoying a varied diet of plant-based whole foods can still easily meet your daily protein needs. Here is a list of amazing protein sources for vegetarians.

1. **LEGUMES AND PULSES** ▸ Legumes are plants that produce a pod with seeds—the seeds are called pulses. This family includes lentils, peas, chickpeas, fava beans, lima beans, soybeans, peanuts, and all the types of beans you can find in the supermarket.

2. **NUTS** ▸ Pistachios, cashews, almonds, Brazil nuts, pecans, and walnuts are all packed with protein, fiber, vitamins, minerals, and healthy fats.

3. **SEEDS** ▸ Pumpkin, sunflower, hemp, chia, sesame, and flax seeds all may be tiny, but they sure pack a nutritional punch. They're filled with protein, fiber, vitamins, and minerals.

4. **NUT AND SEED BUTTERS** ▸ Peanut, cashew, almond, and sunflower seed butters and tahini are great protein sources. They are versatile and used in many of the dishes in this book.

5. **WHOLE GRAINS** ▸ Spelt, teff, barley, sorghum, fonio, farro, freekeh, buckwheat, wild rice, millet, amaranth, and quinoa are all naturally high in iron, B vitamins, fiber, and protein.

6. **BREADS MADE FROM SPROUTED GRAINS** ▸ Sprouting increases the amino acids in grains, which creates a bread that's higher in protein. One popular brand is Ezekiel bread from Food for Life.

7. **SOY** ▸ Tofu, tempeh, and edamame are all sources of complete protein, meaning they contain all nine essential amino acids—amino acids your body cannot synthesize and must get from food.

8. **OATS AND OATMEAL** ▸ Oats are rich in fiber, magnesium, iron, and zinc, but did you know they also contain protein? Oats contain avenalin, a protein not found in other grains but similar to the protein in legumes.

9. **EGGS** ▸ Also a complete source of protein, eggs used to have a bad reputation, but new research has revealed no relationship between the intake of dietary cholesterol and an increase in serum cholesterol. Eggs are a good source of vitamin D and choline, as well as the antioxidants lutein and zeaxanthin, which support eye health.

10. **DAIRY** ▸ Greek yogurt and cottage cheese both contain casein protein. Casein is slowly absorbed by the body, promoting muscle gain and helping prevent muscle breakdown.

Stocking Your Vegetarian Kitchen with Clean Foods

Stocking your kitchen with clean, whole foods, and not heavily processed ones, is a good start for success in your journey to optimal health. When your kitchen is stocked with the essential staples, preparing vegetarian, eating-clean meals will be much easier.

Start by looking through your pantry, refrigerator, and freezer and reading the food labels. Even items you know are vegetarian may not be healthy options. Reading labels is important to identify foods that are high in refined sugar, sodium, unhealthy oils, artificial sweeteners and colors, and preservatives. Toss the heavily processed foods to make room for the items that fit well in an eating-clean vegetarian lifestyle.

Listed below are some must-have staples. Stock up, and you'll always have the ingredients for a quick and easy meal on hand.

The items in your pantry are typically the nonperishable items you can buy in bulk. Remember to always check the sell-by dates and store the older products in the front, to be used up first.

Grains and Pasta
Look for the whole-grain stamp on grains—and a certified gluten-free label on oats if that is an issue for you.

- Amaranth
- Barley
- Buckwheat
- Bulgur
- Brown rice
- Chickpea pasta
- Chickpea rice
- Farro
- Freekeh
- Lentil pasta
- Lentil rice
- Oats, rolled
- Quinoa
- Sorghum
- Whole wheat pasta
- Wild rice

Beans and Legumes

Canned are easier to use, but things like lentils and split peas do cook up quickly from dried. Choose canned products with no added salt.

- Black beans
- Cannellini beans
- Chickpeas
- Great northern beans
- Lentils, red and green
- Pinto beans
- Red kidney beans
- Split peas, green

Dried Fruit, Nuts, and Seeds

Choose unsweetened, unsalted, and sulfur-free products.

- Almonds
- Blueberries
- Cashews
- Cherries
- Chia seeds
- Cranberries
- Dates
- Figs
- Flaxseed, ground
- Hemp hearts (hulled hemp seeds)
- Pecans
- Pine nuts
- Pistachios
- Pumpkin seeds
- Raisins
- Sesame seeds
- Sunflower seeds
- Walnuts

Canned and Jarred Vegetables and Fruit

Choose products with no added sugar or salt.

- Applesauce
- Chipotle peppers
- Coconut milk, light
- Green chiles
- Tomatoes, diced
- Tomato paste
- Tomato puree
- Tomato sauce
- Vegetable stock

Baking Goods

Flour will stay fresh on the shelf for 8 months in a sealed, airtight container.

- Almond extract
- Almond flour, super-fine
- Baking powder, aluminum-free
- Baking soda
- Chocolate chips, dark (70% cacao)
- Cocoa powder, unsweetened
- Gluten-free sorghum blend flour
- Honey
- Maple syrup
- Matcha
- Nutritional yeast
- Vanilla extract
- White whole wheat flour
- Whole wheat flour

continues ▶

Oils and Vinegars

- Apple cider vinegar
- Avocado oil
- Balsamic vinegar
- Nonstick cooking spray, avocado or olive oil
- Olive oil, extra-virgin
- Rice vinegar, unseasoned
- Sesame oil

Spices and Dried Herbs

For spices you do not use often, buy a smaller container. Spices typically will stay fresh for up to 4 years.

- Basil
- Black pepper
- Cardamom
- Cayenne
- Chai spice mix
- Chili powder
- Cinnamon, ground
- Cumin, ground
- Curry powder
- Dill
- Everything bagel seasoning
- Garlic powder
- Onion powder
- Oregano
- Paprika, regular and smoked
- Parsley
- Sea salt
- Turmeric, ground

REFRIGERATOR

Keep your refrigerator well organized to prevent foods from spoiling before you get to eating them. Use the crisper drawer for fresh fruit and vegetables. A crisper drawer is set for low humidity and is ventilated to let out ethylene gases, allowing produce to stay fresh longer. Below are some staples to keep on hand.

Dairy

Whenever possible, choose organic and reduced-fat (2%) or low-fat (1%) dairy products and grass-fed butter.

- Butter, unsalted
- Cheddar cheese
- Cottage cheese
- Greek yogurt
- Milk
- Mozzarella cheese
- Ricotta cheese

Other Staples

Choose pasture-raised eggs, if possible, soy products made with non-GMO soybeans, unsweetened dairy alternatives, and nut and seed butters with no added sugar or salt.

- Eggs
- Lentils, cooked
- Milk alternatives: almond, coconut, oat, soy
- Nondairy cheese alternatives, such as vegetarian parmesan
- Nut and seed butters

- Olives
- Orange juice
- Tahini
- Tofu, extra-firm

Vegetables

For quick and easy prep, look for chopped vegetables in bags. Whenever possible, buy organic produce. Here are some vegetables you may want to have on hand, but focus on what's in season and what you like.

- Brussels sprouts
- Butternut squash
- Carrots
- Fresh herbs: basil, cilantro, mint, parsley
- Garlic
- Leafy greens: arugula, kale, romaine lettuce, spinach
- Mushrooms
- Onions, red and yellow
- Radishes
- Scallions
- Yellow squash
- Zucchini

Fruits

Again, whenever possible, buy organic produce. To cut down on your prep time, wash and cut up fruit, such as berries, mangos, and watermelon, and store in clear containers in the refrigerator. Here are some fruits you may want to have on hand, but focus on what's in season and what you like.

- Apples
- Avocados
- Bananas
- Berries: blueberries, raspberries, strawberries
- Lemons
- Limes
- Mangos
- Oranges
- Pomegranate seeds
- Watermelon

Condiments

Look for condiments with no added sugars and low salt.

- Coconut aminos
- Dijon mustard
- Enchilada sauce
- Hot sauce
- Tamari, 50% reduced-sodium

continues ▶

The freezer is the perfect place to store things like precooked grains, out-of-season fruit, and leftovers for future meals. During the summer months, I stock up on fresh berries to freeze for when they are not in season. Freezing cooked grains is a quick way to get meals on the table, especially grains that take longer to cook, like whole-grain sorghum. I also freeze extra cut vegetables and batch-cooked meals.

Vegetables

Purchasing frozen vegetables is a fast and easy way to add more vegetables to dishes. You can swap out any of the fresh vegetables in the recipes for frozen vegetables.

- Cauliflower rice
- Corn
- Edamame
- Green peas

Fruits

Frozen fruit is a good option to enjoy fruits that are no longer in season. Whenever possible, buy organic frozen fruit. Here are some fruits you may want to keep on hand.

- Berries, mixed
- Blueberries, wild
- Cherries
- Mango, chunks
- Pineapple, chunks
- Strawberries

Grains

Whole grains can be stored in the freezer for up to 1 year. Save time with meal prep and purchase frozen cooked whole grains or batch-cook yourself to store for quick meals.

- Brown rice, cooked
- Corn tortillas
- Flour tortillas, whole-grain
- Naan bread, whole-grain
- Sandwich rolls, whole-grain

How Processed Is Too Processed?

Processed foods are convenient, but when are they *too* processed? Processed food is any food that is altered from its natural state. That may include whole foods that are sliced, chopped, cooked, canned, or frozen. These items are minimally processed. Minimally processed foods still retain their nutrients and still fit in the eating-clean vegetarian lifestyle. Things like pasta are also processed—but also still great for this lifestyle.

The problem arises when foods are heavily processed, meaning they are drastically altered nutritionally. Heavily processed foods have long lists of ingredients that reveal high amounts of sodium, refined sugars, unhealthy oils, artificial sweeteners and colors, as well as preservatives. (Watch out for anything that you can't easily identify as an actual food item.) Heavily processed foods are also lower in nutritional quality and possibly higher in fat and calories. They are best avoided.

Kitchen Equipment

When you have the right tools in your kitchen, you'll be able to prepare your favorite eating-clean vegetarian recipes in a flash. This is a list of the equipment I use most often. You'll need most of these items to make the recipes in this book.

BAKING DISHES

A standard 13-by-9-inch glass baking dish should be in every kitchen. It is perfect for baked French toast, casseroles, or a vegetable lasagna. An 8-by-8-inch baking dish is also handy for smaller dishes such as desserts.

OVEN-SAFE SKILLET OR CAST-IRON SKILLET

A 10- or 12-inch oven-safe skillet is one of the most versatile kitchen tools. It can easily go from the stovetop to the oven and distributes heat evenly when cooking. I recommend using a stainless steel, cast-iron, or enameled cast-iron version. Plain, unenameled cast-iron skillets can even increase your intake of iron, an essential mineral.

DUTCH OVEN OR SOUP POT

A 5- to 7-quart pot is a must-have piece of kitchen equipment. My favorite is a Dutch oven. Once you cook in a Dutch oven, you may never want to be without one! This heavy pot has thick walls and a tight-fitting lid and can be used on the stovetop or in the oven. I definitely recommend making the investment in a ceramic-lined pot with a nonstick surface, which makes for quick cleanup.

BAKING SHEET

A 13-by-18-inch rimmed baking sheet is another one of my favorite pieces of kitchen equipment. An aluminum version lined with unbleached parchment paper or a silicone baking mat stops food from sticking and makes for easy cleanup.

CHEF'S KNIFE

Most recipes require dicing and chopping fresh vegetables. An 8- or 10-inch chef's knife will do just about any job you need. A sharp knife is safer than a dull one, so make sure to give your knives proper maintenance.

CUTTING BOARD

An 18-inch wood or polypropylene board is best, although any size and material will work. I place a damp kitchen towel under my cutting board to prevent it from slipping on the kitchen counter.

SALAD CHOPPER

This is an inexpensive gadget you'll soon find you cannot live without. I use a salad chopper to create bite-size vegetables that are more appealing, especially for kids. There are many varieties, but my favorite type is similar to scissors and can be used with one hand.

HIGH-POWERED BLENDER AND FOOD PROCESSOR

A high-powered blender and a food processor will create the perfect consistency for smoothies, sauces, pesto, and hummus. Both of these are an investment, but one you'll find is worth it for all of your eating-clean vegetarian dishes. A mini food processor is more affordable and can be used for smaller batches of most recipes.

About the Recipes

You're almost ready to dive into the recipes. But first, I want to share with you how to navigate this book. All the recipes are plant-based, meaning they focus on foods primarily from plants. The recipes include lacto-ovo-vegetarian dishes. This means they exclude meat, poultry, seafood, gelatin, and rennet, as well as stock or fat from animals, but may include eggs, dairy products, and honey.

I have labeled the recipes to note that are vegan, dairy-free, gluten-free, nut-free, or soy-free, and I provide tips to swap out ingredients to accommodate some dietary restrictions. I also call out which recipes can be prepared in 30 minutes or less, as well as recipes made in one pot, skillet, or baking sheet for easy cleanup. I hope you are excited to jump into an eating-clean vegetarian lifestyle. Let's get started!

V VEGAN   DF DAIRY-FREE

NF NUT-FREE   GF GLUTEN-FREE

SF SOY-FREE   30 30-MIN OR <

OP ONE POT / SKILLET / PAN

Bulgur and Lentil Salad ▸ 68

CHAPTER 2

YOUR 7-DAY VEGETARIAN EATING-CLEAN JUMP-START

Are you new to eating clean or a vegetarian diet? This 7-day jump-start plan for clean vegetarian meals will help set you up to begin a healthier lifestyle. This plan will introduce you to how delicious and enjoyable eating-clean vegetarian dishes can be. The recipes and snacks in this book include a variety of plant-based whole foods and are satisfying and well balanced. Let's get you started on your journey to feeling great!

About the Meal Plan

When you set out to make a lifestyle change, it's much easier to start with baby steps. I get it. I've made many changes in my own life, and I've helped many clients make positive health changes. I'm here to help you, too.

The simple 7-day plan on page 22 takes the guesswork out of meal planning. The plan includes three meals per day, along with two snacks, to keep you feeling satisfied and excited to cook the next dish. (Or swap your snacks for the optional snacks and desserts listed in the pink bubble next to the chart on page 23.) All the recipes are in this book, and I've allowed for leftovers, so some of the meals and snacks later in the week will come right out of your refrigerator ready to eat.

I have included a shopping list for the week to make your trip to the grocery store a breeze. Be sure to check your pantry and refrigerator for items you already have, then bring this book along with you to the store or take a photo of the shopping list.

A few of the recipes can be made the night before for a quick meal the next day, and many can be enjoyed either warmed or chilled. Snacks can also be prepared ahead of time to enjoy throughout the week or are simple purchases that are already on the shopping list.

Many dishes can be customized to meet your preferences and needs as well. Check out the Variation tips at the end of many of the recipes; they list simple swaps for allergies and intolerances. Are you ready?

The 7-Day Jump-Start Meal Plan

	BREAKFAST	SNACK	LUNCH	SNACK	DINNER
DAY 1	Broccoli and Tomato Crustless Quiche *(page 45)*	¼ cup almonds	Chickpea "No Tuna" Salad *(page 67)* on whole-grain bread	Toasted Quinoa Energy Bites *(page 102)*	Chipotle Cauliflower-Pistachio Tacos *(page 86)* with Avocado Crema *(page 129)*
DAY 2	Berry Chia Overnight Oats *(page 37)*	*Leftover* Toasted Quinoa Energy Bites	*Leftover* Broccoli and Tomato Crustless Quiche	Balsamic Strawberries with Mint *(page 48)*	Baked Penne with Eggplant Ragù *(page 85)*
DAY 3	Egg-in-a-Hole Avocado Toast *(page 41)*	Roasted Garlic and White Bean Spread *(page 124)* with vegetable sticks	*Leftover* Chipotle Cauliflower-Pistachio Taco mixture with mixed greens and *Leftover* Avocado Crema	*Leftover* Toasted Quinoa Energy Bites	Black Bean Falafel with Chipotle Tahini Dressing *(page 87)* in a whole-grain pita with mixed greens

**OPTIONAL
SNACKS OR DESSERTS**

Carrot Cake Muffins *(page 114)*,
Oat Fig Squares *(page 108)*,
Peanut Butter Oatmeal
Cookies *(page 111)*

	BREAKFAST	SNACK	LUNCH	SNACK	DINNER
DAY 4	*Leftover* Berry Chia Overnight Oats	*Leftover* Roasted Garlic and White Bean Spread with vegetable sticks	*Leftover* Chickpea "No Tuna" Salad over mixed greens	¼ cup almonds	Smoky Three-Bean Chili *(page 76)* with a hearty slice of whole-grain bread
DAY 5	Wild Blueberry and Cauliflower Smoothies *(page 33)*	*Leftover* Toasted Quinoa Energy Bites	*Leftover* Black Bean Falafel with Chipotle Tahini Dressing over mixed greens	1 orange or fruit of choice	*Leftover* Smoky Three-Bean Chili over brown rice
DAY 6	Baked Cherry Oatmeal *(page 38)*	½ cup blueberries or fruit of choice	*Leftover* Baked Penne with Eggplant Ragù	1 cup popcorn	Skillet Pizza with Pumpkin Seed Pesto *(page 82)*
DAY 7	*Leftover* Baked Cherry Oatmeal	1 small apple or fruit of choice	*Leftover* Skillet Pizza with Pumpkin Seed Pesto	¼ cup roasted pumpkin seeds	Butternut Squash Lasagna *(page 95)*

Shopping List

Be sure to check your pantry for items you already have on hand before heading to the store, and always check expiration dates for freshness. Where I haven't specified an amount, just buy a box, bottle, jar, or package. (I haven't included the ingredients for the optional desserts, so if you decide to add them, be sure to add those ingredients to your shopping list.)

Cans and Jars

- Beans, black, low-sodium, 3 (15-ounce) cans
- Beans, cannellini, low-sodium, 1 (15-ounce) can
- Beans, great northern, low-sodium, 1 (15-ounce) can
- Beans, red kidney, low-sodium, 1 (15-ounce) can
- Chickpeas, low-sodium, 1 (15-ounce) can
- Chipotle peppers in adobo sauce, 1 small can
- Kalamata olives, ¼ cup sliced
- Tomato puree, no-salt-added, 1 (28-ounce) can
- Tomato basil pasta sauce, low-sodium, no-added-sugar, 2 (24-ounce) jars
- Tomatoes, diced, fire-roasted, no-salt-added, 1 (28-ounce) can and 1 (14.5-ounce) can

Pantry

- Baking powder, aluminum-free
- Black pepper
- Chili powder
- Cinnamon, ground
- Cumin, ground
- Everything bagel seasoning
- Garlic powder
- Honey
- Maple syrup
- Mustard, Dijon
- Nonstick cooking spray
- Nutritional yeast
- Olive oil, extra-virgin
- Paprika, regular
- Paprika, smoked
- Popcorn
- Sea salt
- Vanilla extract, pure
- Vegetable stock, low-sodium
- Vinegar, apple cider
- Vinegar, balsamic
- Vinegar, red wine
- Yeast, active dry, 1 envelope

Pasta, Breads, Grains, and Flours

- Bread, whole-grain, 4 slices
- Corn tortillas, 12 (6-inch)
- Flour, white whole wheat, 2¼ cups
- Lasagna noodles, lentil, oven-ready, 1 (8-ounce) box
- Oats, old-fashioned rolled, 3¾ cups
- Penne pasta, lentil, 1 (8-ounce) box
- Quinoa, ¼ cup

Nuts, Seeds, and Dried Fruit

- Almonds, ¾ cup
- Chia seeds, ¼ cup
- Coconut, unsweetened shredded
- Dates, pitted, 3
- Flaxseed, ground
- Hemp hearts, 6 tablespoons
- Peanut butter, creamy, no-added-sugar, ½ cup
- Pistachios
- Pumpkin seeds, 2½ cups
- Tahini, ¼ cup
- Walnuts

Freezer

- Berries, mixed, ½ cup
- Blueberries, 1 cup
- Cauliflower rice, 1 cup
- Cherries, tart, 1 cup

Refrigerator

- Almond milk, unsweetened vanilla, 3½ cups
- Eggs, 1 dozen
- Lentils, cooked, 1 (9-ounce) package
- Oat milk, unsweetened vanilla, 1 cup

Dairy

- Cheese, mild cheddar, reduced-fat (2%), 1 cup shredded
- Cheese, mozzarella, part-skim, 3 cups shredded
- Cheese, ricotta, part-skim, 3 cups
- Cottage cheese, 2%, ½ cup
- Greek yogurt, 2%, 1 cup
- Milk, 2%, ¾ cup

Fresh Herbs

- Basil, 1 bunch
- Cilantro, 2 bunches
- Mint, 1 bunch
- Parsley, 2 bunches

Fruit

- Apple, 1
- Avocados, 5
- Banana, 1
- Blueberries, ½ cup
- Lemons, 5
- Limes, 3
- Orange, 1
- Strawberries, 1 pound

Vegetables

- Bell pepper, red, 1
- Broccoli, 1 head
- Butternut squash cubes, 1 (20-ounce) package
- Carrots, 1 pound
- Cauliflower, 1 head
- Celery, 2 stalks
- Cherry tomatoes, 2 cups
- Eggplant, 1
- Garlic, 3 heads
- Mixed greens, 2 cups
- Mushrooms, baby bella, 3 (8-ounce) packages

continues ▶

- Onions, red, 2
- Onions, sweet, 2
- Onions, yellow, 3
- Scallions, 1 bunch
- Spinach, baby, 2 cups
- Yellow squash, 1
- Zucchini, 1

Beyond the Seven Days

Congratulations on completing the 7-Day Vegetarian Eating-Clean Jump-Start! Eating this way for a full week is an important step to living a healthier lifestyle. The next six chapters of this book provide a variety of meals and snacks, so you can create your own weekly plans. Many recipes include tips on how to make them ahead, how to store leftovers for later in the week, or how to freeze them for a quick meal when time is tight.

You are now ready to continue your journey by creating your own meal plan with the many recipes in this cookbook. Take the time to review how you want to stock your vegetarian kitchen with the healthy foods discussed in chapter 1 and try to keep the staples on hand for convenience and ease. The tips that follow will help guide you in creating your own meal plans. Use the blank meal plan and grocery list on page 28 to start planning.

Take time to make your plan. Set aside time each week to plan for the week ahead. Creating your weekly meal plan and writing out your shopping list will help keep you on track. Designate a specific day to plan and shop to stay consistent on your journey.

Plan for variety. Choose a variety of dishes for each day and week. The more variety of colorful fruits and vegetables, whole grains, and legumes, the more opportunity to ensure you are meeting your nutritional needs. Choosing dishes that use a variety of foods will also prevent boredom and make your meals more exciting.

Don't forget to hydrate. Remember to add beverages to your meal plan. The most important one is water. Water should be a part of every healthy eating plan. When you start a vegetarian eating-clean meal plan, you will be increasing the amount of fiber you consume, so you'll need plenty of water for healthy digestion. If you find water boring, try adding sliced fruit to your water glass, or fresh herbs such as mint, to add a hint of flavor and make it more interesting.

Store leftovers for additional meals. Portion out your leftovers and pack them in airtight containers to be stored for meals later in the week or to be frozen for weeks ahead. Portioning in individual containers will allow you to grab only what you need for the next meal.

Prep in advance. When you have more time, prepare ingredients for other meals you've planned for the week. Chop vegetables and cook extra grains to store in the refrigerator or the freezer. You can also purchase precut vegetables and frozen cooked grains. Making the sauces and dressings in chapter 8 ahead of time will also save you valuable time in the kitchen later.

	BREAKFAST	SNACK	LUNCH	SNACK	DINNER
DAY 1					
DAY 2					
DAY 3					
DAY 4					
DAY 5					
DAY 6					
DAY 7					

CANS & JARS

_____

_____

_____

_____

_____

PANTRY

_____

_____

_____

_____

PASTA, GRAINS & FLOURS

_____

_____

_____

_____

_____

NUTS & SEEDS

_____

_____

DAIRY

_____

_____

FREEZER

_____

_____

_____

_____

REFRIGERATOR

_____

_____

_____

_____

_____

FRUITS & VEGETABLES

_____

_____

_____

_____

_____

_____

_____

FRESH HERBS

_____

_____

_____

CHAPTER 3

SMOOTHIES AND BREAKFASTS

PINEAPPLE-COCONUT SMOOTHIES

SERVES 2   **PREP TIME** 5 minutes

Pineapples have a long history as a natural health remedy. They contain the enzyme bromelain, which works as an anti-inflammatory to help support a healthy immune system and protect against cardiovascular disease. Pineapples are in season from spring to summer, but when they're out of season, you can enjoy frozen pineapple. Both fresh and frozen work well in this smoothie. If you're using fresh pineapple, simply add 2 or 3 ice cubes.

1½ cups unsweetened
   vanilla coconut milk

½ cup 2% vanilla
   Greek yogurt

1 tablespoon
   ground flaxseed

3 tablespoons hemp hearts

1 teaspoon pure
   vanilla extract

1 tablespoon unsweetened
   shredded coconut

¾ cup frozen
   pineapple chunks

½ cup frozen
   mango chunks

½ medium banana

In a high-powered blender, combine the coconut milk, yogurt, flaxseed, hemp hearts, vanilla, shredded coconut, pineapple, mango, and banana and blend until smooth. Pour into 2 tall glasses. Serve immediately.

TIME SAVER: *Combine all the ingredients except the milk in an airtight container or resealable plastic bag and store in the freezer. Simply empty the bag into your blender and add the milk for a quick smoothie when time is tight.*

PER SERVING: Calories: 295; Protein: 13g; Carbohydrates: 40g; Fiber: 4g; Total fat: 11g; Saturated fat: 1g; Sugar: 29g; Sodium: 132mg

WILD BLUEBERRY AND CAULIFLOWER SMOOTHIES

SERVES 2   **PREP TIME** 5 minutes

Cauliflower in a smoothie? Yes, that's right! Cauliflower adds a creamy consistency and fiber, as well as vitamins C and B, all with a neutral taste. For a protein boost, there's cottage cheese—another unexpected smoothie add-in with a neutral taste. The addition of both will bulk up this smoothie to keep you feeling satisfied longer.

1 cup unsweetened vanilla
  oat milk

3 tablespoons hemp hearts

1 teaspoon pure
  vanilla extract

½ cup 2% cottage cheese

1 cup frozen cauliflower rice

1 cup frozen wild
  blueberries

½ medium banana

1½ tablespoons honey

In a high-powered blender, combine the oat milk, hemp hearts, vanilla, cottage cheese, cauliflower, blueberries, banana, and honey and blend until smooth. Pour into 2 tall glasses. Serve immediately.

INGREDIENT TIP: *Keeping frozen cauliflower rice stocked in your freezer makes for a quick and easy add-in to smoothies, as well as stir-fries, stews, soups, and bowls.*

PER SERVING: Calories: 315; Protein: 12g; Carbohydrates: 44g; Fiber: 5g; Total fat: 12g; Saturated fat: 1g; Sugar: 28g; Sodium: 255mg

MATCHA GREEN TEA SMOOTHIES

SERVES 2 **PREP TIME** 5 minutes

Have you heard of matcha? The word means powdered tea. It's made from green tea leaves that have been dried and stone-ground into a fine powder. Matcha is an antioxidant-dense drink. And since you are drinking the whole leaves, rather than just steeping them to make a cup of tea, it will also be higher in caffeine, providing a healthy boost in the morning.

1 cup unsweetened
  oat milk

¾ cup 2% plain
  Greek yogurt

1 tablespoon
  matcha powder

1 tablespoon chia seeds

3 tablespoons hemp hearts

1 teaspoon pure
  vanilla extract

½ cup frozen
  mango chunks

1 large banana

1 cup baby spinach

1½ tablespoons honey

In a high-powered blender, combine the oat milk, yogurt, matcha, chia seeds, hemp hearts, vanilla, mango, banana, spinach, and honey and blend until smooth. Pour into 2 tall glasses. Serve immediately.

INGREDIENT TIP: *There are two main grades of matcha, ceremonial and culinary, and both work well in smoothies. Ceremonial grade is best when enjoying a cup of matcha tea; it's the highest quality and requires less sweetener. Culinary grade is not as vibrantly green and is less expensive.*

PER SERVING: Calories: 361; Protein: 12g; Carbohydrates: 54g; Fiber: 5g; Total fat: 18g; Saturated fat: 2g; Sugar: 34g; Sodium: 128mg

ALMOND BUTTER AND STRAWBERRY SMOOTHIE BOWLS

SERVES 4 **PREP TIME** 5 minutes

Smoothies are the ultimate on-the-go meal, but a smoothie bowl is great to savor and enjoy when you have a bit more time. Make this bowl your own or get the entire family involved. Customize your bowl with a variety of toppings, including fruit, nuts, and seeds.

2½ cups unsweetened vanilla almond milk

2 tablespoons ground flaxseed

1 teaspoon pure vanilla extract

¼ teaspoon ground cinnamon

2 cups frozen strawberries

1 cup 2% plain Greek yogurt

¼ cup no-added-sugar almond butter

½ medium banana

TOPPINGS

½ medium banana, sliced

2 tablespoons hemp hearts

2 tablespoons unsweetened shredded coconut

¼ cup sliced strawberries, fresh or frozen

1. In a high-powered blender, combine the almond milk, flaxseed, vanilla, cinnamon, strawberries, yogurt, almond butter, and banana and blend until smooth.

2. Pour into four bowls and divide the toppings evenly. Serve immediately.

VARIATION: *For a thicker consistency, add ¼ cup of ice.*

PER SERVING: Calories: 289; Protein: 12g; Carbohydrates: 23g; Fiber: 6g; Total fat: 17g; Saturated fat: 3g; Sugar: 15g; Sodium: 107 mg

CHOCOLATE AND PEANUT BUTTER SMOOTHIE BOWLS

SERVES 4   **PREP TIME** 15 minutes

Chocolate plus peanut butter is the perfect combination, don't you agree? This typical candy combo creates a healthy, balanced morning start with the addition of chia seeds, oats, and Greek yogurt. To make this bowl photo-worthy, heat an additional 2 tablespoons peanut butter in the microwave until it's melted and pourable, then drizzle artfully over the bowl.

2 tablespoons chia seeds

1 cup unsweetened vanilla almond milk

¼ cup old-fashioned rolled oats

1 cup 2% plain Greek yogurt

¼ cup no-added-sugar creamy peanut butter

1 medium banana

2 tablespoons unsweetened cocoa powder

1 teaspoon pure vanilla extract

¼ teaspoon ground cinnamon

½ cup ice cubes

TOPPINGS

½ medium banana, sliced

¼ cup dairy-free dark chocolate chips

2 teaspoons chia seeds

1 tablespoon unsweetened shredded coconut

1. In a small bowl, combine the chia seeds and almond milk and set aside for 10 minutes.

2. Meanwhile, in a high-powered blender, pulse the oats until fine.

3. When the chia seeds are soaked, add them to the oats in the blender along with the yogurt, peanut butter, banana, cocoa powder, vanilla, cinnamon, and ice and blend until smooth.

4. Pour into four bowls and divide the toppings evenly between them. Serve immediately.

VARIATION: *Make this smoothie bowl vegan by switching out the Greek yogurt for a plant-based yogurt.*

PER SERVING: Calories: 308; Protein: 11g; Carbohydrates: 32g; Fiber: 8g; Total fat: 18g; Saturated fat: 6g; Sugar: 14g; Sodium: 65mg

BERRY CHIA OVERNIGHT OATS

SERVES 4 **PREP TIME** 5 minutes, plus 8 hours

Prepping your breakfast the night before can make busy mornings a little easier. Overnight oats are perfect to make ahead and store in airtight containers for up to 4 days. For variety, customize the toppings each day.

¼ cup chia seeds

2 cups unsweetened vanilla almond milk

1 cup old-fashioned rolled oats

1 tablespoon ground flaxseed

3 tablespoons hemp hearts

1 teaspoon pure vanilla extract

2 tablespoons pure maple syrup

¼ teaspoon ground cinnamon

⅛ teaspoon sea salt

TOPPINGS

½ cup 2% plain Greek yogurt

½ cup frozen mixed berries

1 tablespoon unsweetened shredded coconut

1. In a medium bowl, combine the chia seeds, almond milk, oats, flaxseed, hemp hearts, vanilla, maple syrup, cinnamon, and salt. Transfer to four jars or glasses, cover, and refrigerate for 8 hours, or up to 3 days, until you're ready to enjoy.

2. Before eating, in a blender, combine the yogurt and mixed berries and pulse until they're blended. Divide the mixture evenly among the jars or glasses. Top each with shredded coconut.

LEFTOVERS TIP: *Add leftover blended berries and yogurt to any smoothies or smoothie bowl or use it to top the Blueberry and Banana French Toast Bake (page 42).*

PER SERVING: Calories: 330; Protein: 15g; Carbohydrates: 35g; Fiber: 9g; Total fat: 16g; Saturated fat: 1g; Sugar: 12g; Sodium: 117mg

BAKED CHERRY OATMEAL

SERVES 4   **PREP TIME** 5 minutes   **COOK TIME** 35 minutes

Prepping this dish is quick and easy, and you probably already have most of the ingredients in your pantry. Bake this when there's a little more time in the morning and you have no excuses for skipping breakfast.

Nonstick cooking spray

2 cups old-fashioned rolled oats

1¼ teaspoons aluminum-free baking powder

½ teaspoon sea salt

2 large eggs, beaten

1½ cups unsweetened vanilla almond milk

2 teaspoons pure vanilla extract

1 teaspoon ground cinnamon

2 tablespoons unsweetened shredded coconut

1 cup frozen tart cherries

3 tablespoons pure maple syrup (optional)

1. Preheat the oven to 375°F. Mist an 8-by-8-inch baking dish with cooking spray.

2. In a large bowl, combine the oats, baking powder, salt, eggs, almond milk, vanilla, cinnamon, coconut, and cherries.

3. Pour the mixture into the baking dish and bake, uncovered, for 35 minutes, or until the oats are tender and the mixture is set.

4. Allow to cool for about 5 minutes. Serve in bowls, topped with maple syrup, if you like.

LEFTOVERS TIP: *Reheat a serving for a quick breakfast during the week or freeze individual portions in airtight containers to enjoy for future meals. To add more moisture, add a splash of vanilla almond milk before reheating.*

PER SERVING: Calories: 250; Protein: 12g; Carbohydrates: 35g; Fiber: 6g; Total fat: 7g; Saturated fat: 2g; Sugar: 6g; Sodium: 229mg

PUMPKIN SEED AND CRANBERRY OATMEAL COOKIES

MAKES 24 cookies   **PREP TIME** 15 minutes   **COOK TIME** 15 minutes

Cookies for breakfast will get anyone's attention. Adding oats, pumpkin seeds, and hemp hearts turns this breakfast treat into a hearty, nutritious breakfast on the go.

30
DF
GF
NF
SF
V

2 cups old-fashioned rolled oats

3 ripe bananas, mashed

1 tablespoon ground flaxseed

1 tablespoon hemp hearts

¼ cup pumpkin seeds

½ teaspoon ground cinnamon

½ cup no-added-sugar sunflower seed butter

½ cup unsweetened dried cranberries

¼ cup dairy-free dark chocolate chips

½ teaspoon sea salt

1. Preheat the oven to 350°F. Line two rimmed baking sheets with unbleached parchment paper.

2. In a large bowl, combine the oats, bananas, flaxseed, hemp hearts, pumpkin seeds, cinnamon, sunflower seed butter, cranberries, chocolate chips, and salt.

3. Scoop up rounded tablespoons of the cookie dough and press to flatten onto the prepared baking sheets to create two dozen 3-inch cookies.

4. Bake for about 12 minutes, or until the cookies are golden brown.

LEFTOVERS TIP: *Bake only half the dough (12 cookies) and save the remaining dough for future baking. Roll the dough into 1-tablespoon balls and store in an airtight container for up to 5 days in the refrigerator or up to 6 months in the freezer.*

PER SERVING (1 COOKIE): Calories: 95; Protein: 3g; Carbohydrates: 11g; Fiber: 2g; Total fat: 5g; Saturated fat: 1g; Sugar: 4g; Sodium: 25mg

APPLE-CINNAMON SKILLET PANCAKE

SERVES 4   **PREP TIME** 15 minutes   **COOK TIME** 20 minutes

White whole wheat flour is made from a hard white wheat that produces a flour lighter in texture, milder in taste, and paler in color than regular whole wheat flour. It's 100% whole grain and has a nutty flavor. Substituting white whole wheat flour for any recipe calling for all-purpose flour adds nutrients and fiber, and you'll never know the difference.

2 tablespoons avocado oil, divided

3 apples, cored, peeled, and sliced

2 teaspoons ground cinnamon

1½ cups white whole wheat flour

1 teaspoon aluminum-free baking powder

¼ teaspoon baking soda

¼ teaspoon sea salt

2 large eggs

¾ cup unsweetened vanilla almond milk

¼ cup pure maple syrup (optional)

1. Preheat the oven to 375°F.

2. In a 12-inch oven-safe skillet, heat 1 tablespoon of avocado oil over medium heat. Add the apples and cinnamon and sauté for 3 minutes, or until tender and browned. Set the skillet of apples aside.

3. In a medium bowl, blend the flour, baking powder, baking soda, and salt.

4. In a separate bowl, mix together the eggs, almond milk, and remaining 1 tablespoon of avocado oil. Gradually stir the flour mixture into the egg mixture. Blend until combined.

5. Pour the pancake mixture over the apples in the skillet, transfer to the oven, and bake for about 20 minutes, or until the fruit is tender and the pancake is lightly browned.

6. Cut into 4 wedges and serve immediately, topped with maple syrup, if desired.

PER SERVING: Calories: 340; Protein: 11g; Carbohydrates: 55g; Fiber: 9g; Total fat: 11g; Saturated fat: 2g; Sugar: 16g; Sodium: 139mg

EGG-IN-A-HOLE AVOCADO TOAST

SERVES 4   **PREP TIME** 5 minutes   **COOK TIME** 10 minutes

Kids will enjoy assembling this breakfast as much as eating it. If you're making only one or two servings, this dish can easily be made in the toaster oven.

4 slices hearty
whole-grain bread

4 large eggs

2 avocados, peeled, pitted,
and sliced

¼ teaspoon sea salt

1 tablespoon everything
bagel seasoning

½ cup sliced cherry
tomatoes

2 tablespoons minced
scallions

1. Preheat the oven to 400°F. Line a rimmed baking sheet with unbleached parchment paper.

2. Using a 3-inch biscuit cutter (or the top of a glass), make a hole in the center of each bread slice. Evenly space the slices on the prepared pan and crack 1 egg into each hole. Lay the cut-out round of bread next to each slice.

3. Bake the toast for 4 minutes, flip the bread rounds only, and bake for another 4 minutes, or until the egg whites have set, but the yolks are still runny.

4. While the toast cooks, in a small bowl, mash together the avocado and salt.

5. Remove the pan from the oven and spread one-quarter of the mashed avocado onto each slice of toast, around the egg. Sprinkle each slice with everything bagel seasoning, then top with the tomato slices and scallions.

6. Serve each avocado toast with a cut-out bread round to dip in the yolk.

INGREDIENT TIP: *Some brands of everything bagel seasoning contain salt. Read the label closely and leave out the sea salt listed in the recipe if it's already added.*

PER SERVING: Calories: 317; Protein: 12g; Carbohydrates: 24g; Fiber: 9g; Total fat: 21g; Saturated fat: 4g; Sugar: 3g; Sodium: 303mg

BLUEBERRY AND BANANA FRENCH TOAST BAKE

SERVES 6 **PREP TIME** 20 minutes **COOK TIME** 45 minutes

I enjoy making this dish on the weekends when I have a little more time in the morning. The aromas will get everyone up and ready for the day.

Nonstick cooking spray

7 large eggs

1½ cups unsweetened vanilla almond milk

1 teaspoon pure vanilla extract

¼ teaspoon pure almond extract

1½ teaspoons ground cinnamon, divided

12 (¾-inch-thick) slices hearty whole-grain bread, cut into 1-inch cubes

1 cup blueberries

1 medium banana, sliced

¼ cup sliced almonds

6 tablespoons pure maple syrup (optional)

1. Preheat the oven to 350°F. Mist a 9-by-13-inch baking dish with cooking spray.

2. In a medium bowl, beat the eggs. Add the almond milk, vanilla, almond extract, and 1 teaspoon of cinnamon and combine well.

3. Spread the cubed bread in the prepared baking dish. Pour the egg mixture over the bread and gently fold until the bread is moistened. Let stand for at least 10 minutes so the bread can soak up the egg mixture.

4. Stir in the blueberries, banana, and almonds. Evenly sprinkle the remaining ½ teaspoon of cinnamon on top. Bake for 45 minutes, or until all the liquid has been absorbed and the bread is golden brown.

5. Divide the French toast bake among six bowls. If desired, drizzle 1 tablespoon of maple syrup over each serving.

TIME SAVER: *Assemble this dish ahead of time and store in the refrigerator overnight, covered with plastic wrap. In the morning, just pop it in the oven and bake.*

....

PER SERVING: Calories: 317; Protein: 12g; Carbohydrates: 24g; Fiber: 9g; Total fat: 21g; Saturated fat: 4g; Sugar: 3g; Sodium: 303mg

SPINACH AND POTATO FRITTATA

GF

NF

SF

SERVES 6   **PREP TIME** 10 minutes   **COOK TIME** 25 minutes

Yes, white potatoes are part of a healthy diet. Yukon Gold potatoes are a variety of white potatoes and are considered an all-purpose potato. They're full of essential nutrients, including iron, vitamin B6, vitamin C, and potassium, as well as being an excellent source of fiber.

2 tablespoons extra-virgin olive oil

½ yellow onion, diced

2 cups diced Yukon Gold potatoes

8 large eggs

¾ cup 2% milk

½ teaspoon sea salt

¼ teaspoon freshly ground black pepper

½ cup shredded reduced-fat (2%) mild cheddar cheese

2 cups packed baby spinach

1. Preheat the oven to 425°F.

2. In a 12-inch oven-safe skillet, heat the olive oil over medium heat. Add the onion and sauté for 3 minutes, or until translucent. Add the potatoes and sauté for 3 minutes, or until they are slightly browned.

3. In a large bowl, mix together the eggs, milk, salt, pepper, cheddar, and spinach.

4. Pour the egg mixture over the potatoes in the skillet, transfer to the oven, and bake for 15 minutes, or until the eggs are set.

5. Cool slightly and cut into 6 wedges.

LEFTOVERS TIP: *Enjoy leftover frittata for lunch wrapped in a tortilla and topped with hot sauce.*

PER SERVING: Calories: 214; Protein: 13g; Carbohydrates: 12g; Fiber: 2g; Total fat: 13g; Saturated fat: 3g; Sugar: 3g; Sodium: 277mg

MUSHROOM BREAKFAST QUESADILLAS

SERVES 2   **PREP TIME** 10 minutes   **COOK TIME** 20 minutes

Mix up breakfast by serving dishes you don't typically think of as morning meals—like this breakfast quesadilla. Add your favorite veggies and top it with salsa or sliced avocado.

2 tablespoons extra-virgin olive oil, divided

1 cup sliced mushrooms

4 large eggs

¼ teaspoon sea salt

⅛ teaspoon freshly ground black pepper

4 (8-inch) corn tortillas

4 tablespoons shredded reduced-fat (2%) Mexican cheese blend

1. In a medium skillet, heat 1 tablespoon of olive oil over medium heat. Add the mushrooms and sauté for 5 minutes.

2. Meanwhile, in a medium bowl, beat the eggs with the salt and pepper.

3. Pour the eggs over the mushrooms and lightly divide the mixture in half, pushing each half to one side of the pan. Cook until the eggs begin to set without being runny, about 3 minutes.

4. Lay 2 tortillas next to each other on a rimmed baking sheet. Add half the egg mixture to each tortilla and sprinkle each with 2 tablespoons of cheese. Top with the remaining 2 tortillas.

5. In the same skillet, heat the remaining 1 tablespoon of olive oil over medium heat. Place a quesadilla in the skillet, cover, and heat for 2 minutes, then flip. Cook, covered for another 2 minutes, until the quesadilla is browned on both sides. Repeat with the second quesadilla. Cut each quesadilla into quarters and serve.

PER SERVING: Calories: 464; Protein: 20g; Carbohydrates: 32g; Fiber: 4g; Total fat: 28g; Saturated fat: 8g; Sugar: 2g; Sodium: 354mg

BROCCOLI AND TOMATO CRUSTLESS QUICHE

SERVES 4   **PREP TIME** 10 minutes   **COOK TIME** 40 minutes

A quiche is the perfect dish to make for brunch when you have a bit more time. The leftovers provide another easy breakfast, or try them over greens for a balanced, satisfying lunch. Switch it up with your favorite vegetables and cheese.

Nonstick cooking spray

6 large eggs

¾ cup 2% milk

½ yellow onion, diced

½ teaspoon sea salt

¼ teaspoon freshly ground black pepper

2 scallions, diced

1 head broccoli, chopped

1 cup halved cherry tomatoes

1 cup shredded reduced-fat (2%) mild cheddar cheese

1. Preheat the oven to 375°F. Mist an 8-by-8-inch baking dish with cooking spray.

2. In a large bowl, whisk together the eggs and milk. Add the onion, salt, pepper, scallions, broccoli, tomatoes, and cheddar. Pour into the prepared dish.

3. Bake for 40 minutes, or until the eggs are set. Cut into 6 slices and serve.

LEFTOVERS TIP: *Freeze individual portions for up to 3 months for quick meals.*

PER SERVING: Per serving: Calories: 239; Protein: 21g; Carbohydrates: 11g; Fiber: 3g; Total fat: 11g; Saturated fat: 5g; Sugar: 6g; Sodium: 512mg

CHAPTER 4

SNACKS AND SIDES

BALSAMIC STRAWBERRIES WITH MINT

SERVES 4 **PREP TIME** 5 minutes, plus 15 minutes to marinate

Strawberries and balsamic vinegar pair beautifully. The tanginess of the vinegar brings out the sweetness of the strawberries. Black pepper added to strawberries is a secret of many chefs and will heighten the flavor even more. Allowing the strawberries to sit for 15 minutes in the balsamic vinegar, honey, and pepper will draw out their natural juices. Add the strawberries to oatmeal, Greek yogurt, or avocado toast.

1 pound strawberries, quartered

2 tablespoons honey

⅛ teaspoon freshly ground black pepper

1½ tablespoons balsamic vinegar

Grated zest of 1 lemon

6 fresh mint leaves

2 tablespoons chopped walnuts (optional)

1. In a nonmetal medium bowl, combine the strawberries, honey, black pepper, and balsamic vinegar. Let the strawberries sit for 15 minutes.

2. Serve in four bowls topped with lemon zest and mint leaves. If desired, add chopped walnuts.

VARIATION: *To make this vegan, use maple syrup or coconut sugar instead of honey.*

PER SERVING: Calories: 76; Protein: 1g; Carbohydrates: 19g; Fiber: 2g; Total fat: 0g; Saturated fat: 0g; Sugar: 15g; Sodium: 3mg

BERRY GUACAMOLE

SERVES 6 **PREP TIME** 10 minutes

I often add berries to my homemade guacamole and always get an unsolicited "Wow!" from my friends and family. I love to add unexpected, nutrient-dense ingredients to more common dishes.

3 avocados, peeled
and pitted

½ teaspoon sea salt

¼ red onion, diced

1 tablespoon minced
fresh cilantro

Juice of 1 lime

¼ cup diced strawberries

¼ cup blueberries

1. Scoop the avocado flesh into a medium bowl and mash with the back of a fork.

2. Add the salt, red onion, cilantro, and lime juice and combine well. Fold in the strawberries and blueberries.

VARIATION: *Use in-season fruit or what you have on hand in place of the berries, such as pomegranate seeds or diced mango, mandarin oranges, or apples.*

PER SERVING: Calories: 170; Protein: 2g; Carbohydrates: 11g; Fiber: 7g; Total fat: 15g; Saturated fat: 2g; Sugar: 2g; Sodium: 104mg

VEGAN CREAMY STREET CORN DIP

SERVES 6   **PREP TIME** 5 minutes   **COOK TIME** 25 minutes

Elote is a popular street food in Mexico, as well as the United States. The grilled corn on the cob is typically served on a stick and covered with a chile-lime Cotija cheese sauce. This version takes all the flavors of street corn and makes it into a fun, flavorful vegan dip. Serve it in a bowl with whole-grain crostini, whole-grain pita chips, or tortilla chips.

1 cup cashews

¼ cup extra-virgin olive oil

¼ cup nutritional yeast

1 tablespoon coconut aminos

¼ teaspoon garlic powder

¼ teaspoon onion powder

Juice of 1 lime

1 teaspoon smoked paprika

2 cups frozen fire-roasted corn, thawed

1 cup canned low-sodium black beans, drained and rinsed

1. Put the cashews in a small saucepan and pour in enough water to cover. Bring to a boil, then reduce the heat and simmer for 20 minutes. Drain.

2. In a food processor, combine the cashews, olive oil, nutritional yeast, coconut aminos, garlic powder, onion powder, lime juice, and smoked paprika and blend until smooth.

3. In a medium saucepan, heat the corn and black beans over medium-low heat. Stir in the cashew mixture and heat through before serving.

VARIATION: *Fire-roasted corn will give this dish that grilled corn taste, but you can also use regular sweet corn.*

....

PER SERVING: Calories: 304; Protein: 9g; Carbohydrates: 28g; Fiber: 5g; Total fat: 20g; Saturated fat: 3g; Sugar: 2g; Sodium: 147mg

SMOKY ROASTED CARROT DIP

SERVES 6 **PREP TIME** 10 minutes **COOK TIME** 30 minutes

Carrots come in a variety of colors, including orange, yellow, white, and even purple. The more common bright orange carrot gets it color from beta-carotene. Carrots are a good source of this antioxidant, which the body converts to vitamin A. Vitamin A promotes healthy vision and a healthy immune system, and is an important vitamin for growth and development in children. This recipe is an easy and tasty dish for the entire family to enjoy with cut-up vegetables or whole-grain pita or naan bread.

1 pound carrots, peeled and quartered crosswise

3 tablespoons avocado oil

¼ cup tahini

½ teaspoon sea salt

2 garlic cloves, minced

1 (15-ounce) can low-sodium chickpeas, drained and rinsed

Juice of 1 lemon

1 teaspoon smoked paprika, plus more for garnish

1 teaspoon ground cumin

3 tablespoons water (optional)

1. Preheat the oven to 425°F. Line a rimmed baking sheet with unbleached parchment paper.

2. Spread the carrots on the prepared baking sheet and roast for 15 minutes. Turn them and continue roasting for 15 minutes more, or until softened and browned.

3. In a food processor, combine the roasted carrots, avocado oil, tahini, salt, garlic, chickpeas, lemon juice, smoked paprika, and cumin. Process until smooth, adding the water if needed to create a smoother consistency.

4. Serve in a bowl garnished with an additional pinch of smoked paprika.

LEFTOVERS TIP: *This dip also makes a great spread. Add it to wraps and panini sandwiches, or on top of salads and grain bowls. Store it in an airtight container in the refrigerator for up to 5 days.*

PER SERVING: Calories: 225; Protein: 6g; Carbohydrates: 22g; Fiber: 6g; Total fat: 14g; Saturated fat: 2g; Sugar: 6g; Sodium: 165mg

SWEET POTATO CAKES

SERVES 4   **PREP TIME** 10 minutes   **COOK TIME** 30 minutes

Sweet potatoes are more perishable than you might think; they're best if used within 7 days. When I have leftover sweet potatoes, I'll make this recipe before they spoil. Enjoy this dish as a quick snack, appetizer, breakfast, or light lunch. Pair it with the Smoky Roasted Carrot Dip (page 51).

1 pound sweet potatoes, peeled and cubed

2 tablespoons pure maple syrup

1 large egg

½ teaspoon ground cinnamon

¼ teaspoon sea salt

⅛ teaspoon freshly ground black pepper

½ cup almond flour

1 tablespoon extra-virgin olive oil

2 tablespoons chopped scallions

1. Bring a medium saucepan of water to a boil. Add the sweet potatoes and cook for 15 minutes, or until tender.

2. Remove from the heat, drain, and place in a large bowl. Mash with a potato masher. Add the maple syrup, egg, cinnamon, salt, black pepper, and almond flour. Combine well.

3. In a medium skillet, heat the olive oil over medium heat. Scoop 3 tablespoons of potato mixture into the pan and press down with the back of a spatula to make a ½-inch-thick patty. Repeat to make additional patties. Cook for 5 minutes on each side, flipping with a spatula.

4. Serve topped with chopped scallions.

TIME SAVER: *Save time by cooking the potatoes in the microwave. Pierce the unpeeled sweet potatoes with a fork on all sides and microwave on high for 8 minutes. When cool enough to handle, peel off the skin and proceed with the recipe as written.*

PER SERVING: Calories: 242; Protein: 6g; Carbohydrates: 33g; Fiber: 5g; Total fat: 11g; Saturated fat: 1g; Sugar: 11g; Sodium: 160mg

GRILLED EGGPLANT WITH LEMON-CUMIN YOGURT SAUCE

30 **GF** **SF**

SERVES 4   **PREP TIME** 10 minutes   **COOK TIME** 20 minutes

Many cooks prefer to peel their eggplant, but the skin is packed with powerful nutrients, such as the antioxidant nasunin, which gives eggplant its purple color. This antioxidant may help protect brain cell membranes from damage caused by free radicals. The peel of a Japanese eggplant is a bit thinner than that of other eggplants, making it easier to cook and enjoy.

4 Japanese egg-
plants, trimmed and
halved lengthwise

1 tablespoon extra-virgin
olive oil

½ teaspoon sea salt

⅛ teaspoon freshly ground
black pepper

1 teaspoon garlic powder

1 tablespoon chopped
fresh parsley

1 tablespoon chopped
fresh basil

¼ cup pine nuts

¼ cup Lemon-Cumin
Yogurt Sauce (page 125)

1. If you have an outdoor grill, preheat it to medium-high. Otherwise, preheat a stovetop grill pan over high heat.

2. In a large bowl, toss together the eggplant, olive oil, salt, black pepper, and garlic powder.

3. Place the eggplant halves on the grill or grill pan and cook for 10 minutes. Flip and cook for another 10 minutes, until golden brown and tender.

4. Place two halves on each plate and top with parsley, basil, and pine nuts. Drizzle the yogurt sauce over the eggplant and serve.

VARIATION: *For an additional nutty flavor, toast the pine nuts before topping the eggplant. Preheat the oven to 350°F. Place the pine nuts in a single layer on a rimmed baking sheet lined with unbleached parchment paper. Bake for 5 minutes, or until golden and fragrant.*

PER SERVING: Calories: 158; Protein: 4g; Carbohydrates: 18g; Fiber: 9g; Total fat: 10g; Saturated fat: 1g; Sugar: 10g; Sodium: 152mg

MAPLE BRUSSELS SPROUTS AND BUTTERNUT SQUASH

SERVES 6   **PREP TIME** 20 minutes   **COOK TIME** 35 minutes

Brussels sprouts are members of the cruciferous vegetable family and are a very nutrient-dense food. They are rich in folate and fiber, and a good source of vitamins A and C. Brussels sprouts are also high in vitamin K, an important nutrient for bone health. Find this cruciferous vegetable in season in the fall through winter and in the freezer section all year round.

1 pound Brussels sprouts, trimmed and roughly chopped

1¼ pounds butternut squash, peeled, seeded, and cut into ½-inch cubes

1 tablespoon avocado oil

½ teaspoon sea salt

⅛ teaspoon freshly ground black pepper

¼ cup unsweetened dried cranberries

2 tablespoons pure maple syrup

¼ cup chopped walnuts

1. Preheat the oven to 425°F. Line a rimmed baking sheet with unbleached parchment paper.

2. In a large bowl, toss together the Brussels sprouts, butternut squash, avocado oil, salt, and pepper.

3. Spread out on the prepared baking sheet and roast for 15 minutes. Flip and stir the vegetables, then roast for another 15 minutes.

4. Add the cranberries, maple syrup, and walnuts and stir to combine well. Roast for another 5 minutes.

TIME SAVER: *Prep this dish by using a food processor to chop the Brussels sprouts. Trim off the stem ends. Feed the sprouts into a food processor fitted with the slicing disc. You can also buy butternut squash and Brussels sprouts already cleaned and precut in the refrigerated section of the produce department.*

PER SERVING: Calories: 148; Protein: 4g; Carbohydrates: 24g; Fiber: 5g; Total fat: 6g; Saturated fat: 1g; Sugar: 7g; Sodium: 120mg

ROASTED CAULIFLOWER WITH GARLIC AND WHITE BEAN SAUCE

DF
GF
NF
SF
V

SERVES 4 **PREP TIME** 10 minutes **COOK TIME** 1 hour

Did you know that cauliflower is packed with vitamin C? Vitamin C is a powerful antioxidant, known for its anti-inflammatory effects that may help protect your body against infection. Just 1 cup of cauliflower can provide more than 75 percent of your daily needs.

1 head cauliflower

3 tablespoons avocado oil

½ teaspoon sea salt

⅛ teaspoon freshly ground black pepper

2 tablespoons chopped fresh parsley, divided

2 tablespoons chopped fresh basil, divided

½ cup Roasted Garlic and White Bean Spread (page 124)

1 teaspoon smoked paprika

2 tablespoons hemp hearts

1. Preheat the oven to 425°F.

2. Remove the leaves from the cauliflower and cut out the core so it stands flat. Place the cauliflower head in a 5-quart Dutch oven.

3. In a small bowl, whisk together the avocado oil, salt, black pepper, and 1 tablespoon each of parsley and basil and pour over the cauliflower head.

4. Cover, transfer to the oven, and roast for 55 minutes.

5. Uncover and place the dish under the broiler for 3 minutes.

6. Place the cauliflower head on a large serving plate. Cover with the roasted garlic and white bean spread, sprinkle with the smoked paprika, and top with the remaining parsley and basil, and the hemp hearts.

VARIATION: *If you don't have a Dutch oven, use a baking dish and cover it with aluminum foil. Uncover for the last 5 minutes to broil.*

PER SERVING: Calories: 214; Protein: 6g; Carbohydrates: 14g; Fiber: 5g; Total fat: 16g; Saturated fat: 2g; Sugar: 3g; Sodium: 227mg

GARLIC-BALSAMIC SAUTÉED MUSHROOMS

SERVES 4   **PREP TIME** 10 minutes   **COOK TIME** 10 minutes

Did you know mushrooms are the only plant-based source of vitamin D? Mushrooms can synthesize vitamin D when exposed to UV light, just as we can. Vitamin D is important for bone health and a healthy immune system. It's primarily found in animal-protein foods, so if you're vegan, mushrooms are the only natural source of vitamin D. Add these mushrooms to tacos, salads, omelets, and grain bowls.

2 tablespoons extra-virgin olive oil

4 garlic cloves, minced

¼ cup balsamic vinegar

1 tablespoon pure maple syrup

1 pound baby bella mushrooms, sliced

¼ teaspoon sea salt

⅛ teaspoon freshly ground black pepper

2 tablespoons chopped fresh parsley, divided

1. In a medium skillet, heat the olive oil over medium heat. Add the garlic, vinegar, maple syrup, mushrooms, salt, black pepper, and 1 tablespoon of parsley. Sauté for 10 minutes, or until lightly browned.

2. Serve topped with the remaining 1 tablespoon of parsley.

LEFTOVERS TIP: *Add leftovers to the Mushroom Breakfast Quesadillas (page 44) or on top of the Root Vegetable Farro Bowls with Green Tahini Sauce (page 75). Double this recipe to have some to add to several dishes throughout the week.*

PER SERVING: Calories: 117; Protein: 4g; Carbohydrates: 11g; Fiber: 1g; Total fat: 7g; Saturated fat: 1g; Sugar: 8g; Sodium: 89mg

ROASTED BROCCOLI WITH CHIPOTLE TAHINI DRESSING

GF

NF

SF

SERVES 4 **PREP TIME** 10 minutes **COOK TIME** 35 minutes

Roasted broccoli adds a boost of fiber and flavor to many dishes. This recipe is easy to prep on the weekend to add to weeknight dishes. Add some sweet and spicy flavor to eggs, on top of avocado toast, in a grain bowl, tossed in a salad, or piled on the Skillet Pizza with Pumpkin Seed Pesto (page 82).

2 large heads broccoli, cut into bite-size florets

1 tablespoon avocado oil

¼ teaspoon sea salt

1 teaspoon garlic powder

⅛ teaspoon freshly ground black pepper

Juice of 1 lemon

¼ cup Chipotle Tahini Dressing (page 132)

2 tablespoons sesame seeds

1. Preheat the oven to 425°F. Line a rimmed baking sheet with unbleached parchment paper.

2. In a large bowl, toss together the broccoli, avocado oil, salt, garlic powder, and black pepper. Transfer to the prepared baking sheet and spread out in a single layer. Roast for 35 minutes, turning after 15 minutes.

3. Remove the broccoli from the oven, squeeze the lemon juice over the top, toss again, and serve topped with the chipotle tahini dressing and sesame seeds.

TIME SAVER: *When shopping for broccoli, look for precut florets in the refrigerated section of the produce department to save time prepping.*

PER SERVING: Calories: 122; Protein: 4g; Carbohydrates: 11g; Fiber: 4g; Total fat: 8g; Saturated fat: 1g; Sugar: 3g; Sodium: 148mg

DELICATA SQUASH WITH GREEN TAHINI SAUCE

SERVES 4   **PREP TIME** 10 minutes   **COOK TIME** 20 minutes

Delicata is a variety of winter squash known for its nutty, sweet taste and edible skin. It's available in the late summer through early winter and can be stored in a cool, dry place for up to 6 months. Roasted delicata squash is very versatile and easy to cook, and can be added to salads, bowls, soups, and stews.

2 medium delicata squash, halved length-wise, seeded, and cut crosswise into ½-inch half-moons

1 tablespoon avocado oil

½ teaspoon sea salt

⅛ teaspoon freshly ground black pepper

¼ cup Green Tahini Sauce (page 127)

¼ cup chopped pistachios

1. Preheat the oven to 425°F. Line a rimmed baking sheet with unbleached parchment paper.

2. In a large bowl, toss the delicata squash, avocado oil, salt, and black pepper. Transfer to the prepared baking sheet and spread out in a single layer. Roast for 20 minutes, turning after 10 minutes.

3. Transfer the cooked squash to a serving plate and top with the green tahini sauce and pistachios.

LEFTOVERS TIP: *Add leftover squash to the Poached Pear and Arugula Salad with Pecans (page 64) or Bulgur and Lentil Salad (page 68).*

PER SERVING: Calories: 220; Protein: 4g; Carbohydrates: 28g; Fiber: 4g; Total fat: 12g; Saturated fat: 4g; Sugar: 3g; Sodium: 183mg

ZUCCHINI BREAD WITH WALNUTS

SERVES 8 **PREP TIME** 15 minutes **COOK TIME** 45 minutes

Gluten-free baked goods have come a long way! But just because a baked good is gluten-free doesn't always mean it includes healthier, nutrient-dense ingredients. Often, more sugar is added or refined grains are used. When you bake your own, you avoid all that. Most conventional grocery stores now carry blends of gluten-free flours that contain buckwheat, sorghum, teff, arrowroot, or brown rice flour. Look for a flour that can be substituted one-for-one for regular wheat flour.

Nonstick cooking spray

2 large eggs

¼ cup pure maple syrup

1 ripe banana, mashed

2 cups gluten-free baking blend

½ teaspoon baking soda

½ teaspoon aluminum-free baking powder

½ teaspoon sea salt

1 teaspoon ground cinnamon

1½ cups shredded zucchini

½ cup chopped walnuts

2 teaspoons grated lemon zest (optional)

1. Preheat the oven to 350°F. Mist a 9-by-5-inch loaf pan with cooking spray.

2. In a large bowl, beat together the eggs, maple syrup, and banana. Set aside.

3. In a medium bowl, combine the baking blend, baking soda, baking powder, salt, and cinnamon.

4. Add half the dry ingredients to the egg mixture and combine. Add the remaining dry ingredients and combine. Fold in the zucchini, walnuts, and lemon zest (if using).

5. Pour the batter into the prepared pan and bake for 45 minutes, or until a toothpick inserted in the center comes out clean. Cool before slicing.

VARIATION: *Look for a gluten-free flour that contains xanthan gum or arrowroot flour. If neither is included in the flour you choose, add 1 teaspoon xanthan gum or arrowroot. This addition will help produce a bread with better texture.*

PER SERVING: Calories: 223; Protein: 6g; Carbohydrates: 36g; Fiber: 2g; Total fat: 6g; Saturated fat: 1g; Sugar: 9g; Sodium: 204mg

Avocado and Citrus Salad ▸ 63

CHAPTER 5

SALADS, SOUPS, AND BOWLS

WATERMELON AND TOMATO SALAD

SERVES 4 **PREP TIME** 10 minutes

Watermelon and tomato combine to make the easiest, most refreshing salad for summer. The crisp, juicy fruit will cool you off on those hot summer afternoons, especially since you don't have to turn on the oven. The peppery and slightly spicy kick of the arugula is complemented by the sweetness of the watermelon and tomatoes.

5 cups cubed watermelon

2 cups packed baby arugula

¼ cup crumbled reduced-fat (2%) feta cheese

8 fresh basil leaves, chopped

1 cup halved mixed medley cherry tomatoes

¼ cup sliced almonds

¼ teaspoon sea salt

⅛ teaspoon freshly ground black pepper

4 tablespoons Honey Balsamic Dressing (page 130)

1. In a large bowl, combine the watermelon, arugula, feta, basil, tomatoes, almonds, salt, and pepper.

2. Divide among four plates and drizzle each salad with 1 tablespoon dressing.

VARIATION: *Make this dish dairy-free by substituting chickpeas for the feta cheese.*

PER SERVING: Calories: 171; Protein: 4g; Carbohydrates: 22g; Fiber: 2g; Total fat: 8g; Saturated fat: 2g; Sugar: 17g; Sodium: 221mg

AVOCADO AND CITRUS SALAD

SERVES 6 **PREP TIME** 15 minutes

Avocado is one of the only fruits loaded with good fats (most fruits contain primarily carbohydrates). Avocados are about 77 percent fat, mainly monounsaturated fats. Unsaturated fats help boost the absorption of fat-soluble vitamins A, D, K, and E. Avocados are also a great source of fiber and potassium.

2 oranges, peeled and cut into ½-inch slices

1 grapefruit, peeled and cut into ½-inch slices

½ small red onion, chopped

2 avocados, peeled, pitted, and cut into ½-inch cubes

1 cucumber, cut into ½-inch cubes

1 (15-ounce) can low-sodium chickpeas, drained and rinsed

¼ cup chopped walnuts

¼ cup Honey Balsamic Dressing (page 130)

In a large bowl, combine the oranges, grapefruit, red onion, avocados, cucumber, chickpeas, walnuts, and dressing. Toss well.

INGREDIENT TIP: *Store citrus fruits on the counter if you plan to eat them within 1 week. Otherwise, keep them in the refrigerator. When stored in the crisper drawer, citrus will stay fresh for up to 3 weeks.*

PER SERVING: Calories: 273; Protein: 6g; Carbohydrates: 28g; Fiber: 9g; Total fat: 17g; Saturated fat: 3g; Sugar: 12g; Sodium: 118mg

POACHED PEAR AND ARUGULA SALAD WITH PECANS

SERVES 4   **PREP TIME** 5 minutes   **COOK TIME** 20 minutes

Bosc pears are one of the more popular types, as they are sweeter and more flavorful than other varieties. In the US, Boscs are grown mostly in Oregon and Washington and are in season from September through the winter. Because of their firmer, denser flesh, they are ideal for baking and poaching. Of course, they're perfect just on their own, too. Anjou and Bartlett pears work especially well for poaching.

1½ cups orange juice

½ teaspoon ground cinnamon

2 firm-ripe Bosc pears, peeled, halved, and cored

1 tablespoon extra-virgin olive oil

2 shallots, sliced

1 (5-ounce) bag baby arugula

¼ cup pecans

¼ cup crumbled reduced-fat (2%) goat cheese

¼ cup pomegranate seeds

½ cup Honey Balsamic Dressing (page 130)

1. In a medium saucepan (or whatever will fit the pears in a single layer), combine the orange juice and cinnamon. Bring to a boil over medium heat. Add the pears to the saucepan cut-side down and simmer for 15 minutes. Remove the pears and set aside. Discard the juice.

2. Heat the olive oil in the same saucepan over medium heat. Add the shallots and sauté for 4 minutes, or until tender and lightly browned. Set aside.

3. In a large bowl, combine the baby arugula, pecans, goat cheese, pomegranate seeds, and dressing and toss well.

4. Divide the mixture among four bowls and top each with a pear half.

VARIATION: *Swap the pomegranate seeds for unsweetened dried cranberries.*

PER SERVING: Calories: 305; Protein: 3g; Carbohydrates: 37g; Fiber: 5g; Total fat: 17g; Saturated fat: 2g; Sugar: 26g; Sodium: 159mg

KALE SALAD WITH GREEN TAHINI DRESSING

SERVES 4 **PREP TIME** 10 minutes

I probably enjoy a kale salad at least once a week. I typically prefer curly kale because the leaves are less firm than lacinato (dinosaur) kale, making it easier to tear off the tough stems and chop the greens for a salad. Many stores sell bagged chopped curly kale, which makes prepping your salad much easier.

5 cups chopped
stemmed kale

½ cup chopped
red cabbage

1 apple, peeled, cored, and
cut into 1-inch cubes

½ red onion, diced

¼ cup sunflower seeds

¼ cup unsweetened
dried cranberries

¼ cup Green Tahini Sauce
(page 127)

In a large bowl, combine the kale, cabbage, apple, onion, sunflower seeds, cranberries, and tahini sauce. Combine well. Divide among four bowls to serve.

VARIATION: *Mandarin orange segments or pears also work well in this salad.*

PER SERVING: Calories: 163; Protein: 4g; Carbohydrates: 18g; Fiber: 3g; Total fat: 10g; Saturated fat: 1g; Sugar: 11g; Sodium: 43mg

CHOPPED RAW SALAD

SERVES 4 **PREP TIME** 15 minutes, plus 20 minutes to marinate

Stocking your kitchen with healthy meal add-ins is a sure way to stay on track with an eating-clean vegetarian lifestyle. Here I cut a variety of raw vegetables into bite-size pieces and marinate them in a red wine vinegar marinade. I often add a scoop of this to other salads, such as the Bulgur and Lentil Salad (page 68), or simply eat it on its own with some hummus and pita.

½ red onion, diced

1 cup quartered
  cherry tomatoes

1 cup bite-size
  cauliflower florets

2 carrots, peeled and cut
  into 1-inch-thick pieces

1 yellow bell pepper,
  chopped

½ cucumber, cut into
  1-inch cubes

½ cup Vegetable Marinade
  (page 120)

2 cups chopped
  romaine lettuce

½ cup ½-inch cubes
  Asiago cheese

1 avocado, peeled, pitted,
  and cut into 1-inch cubes

1. In a large bowl, combine the onion, tomatoes, cauliflower, carrots, bell pepper, cucumber, and marinade. Cover, place in the refrigerator, and marinate for up to 20 minutes.

2. Divide the romaine lettuce among four bowls. Dividing evenly, top with the marinated vegetables, Asiago, and avocado.

VARIATION: *Add ¼ cup pitted sliced olives or ¼ cup of your favorite nuts for an extra boost of healthy fats.*

PER SERVING: Calories: 249; Protein: 7g; Carbohydrates: 18g; Fiber: 7g; Total fat: 18g; Saturated fat: 4g; Sugar: 5g; Sodium: 312mg

CHICKPEA "NO TUNA" SALAD

SERVES 2   **PREP TIME** 10 minutes

This is a great dish to prepare in batches and keep stocked in the refrigerator for quick lunches. Make a classic sandwich by piling it on hearty whole-grain bread with a slice of tomato and crisp lettuce or enjoy in lettuce cups or on top of a green salad.

1 (15-ounce) can low-sodium chickpeas, drained and rinsed

Juice of ½ lemon

¼ cup Roasted Garlic and White Bean Spread (page 124)

½ cup finely chopped celery

¼ red onion, finely chopped

½ teaspoon Dijon mustard

¼ teaspoon sea salt

⅛ teaspoon freshly ground black pepper

1. In a large bowl, mash the chickpeas with a potato masher or the back of a spoon.

2. Add the lemon juice, bean spread, celery, onion, mustard, salt, and pepper. Mix well.

VARIATION: *You can use store-bought hummus or vegan mayonnaise in place of the Roasted Garlic and White Bean Spread.*

PER SERVING: Calories: 220; Protein: 10g; Carbohydrates: 33g; Fiber: 9g; Total fat: 6g; Saturated fat: 0g; Sugar: 6g; Sodium: 468mg

BULGUR AND LENTIL SALAD

SERVES 4 **PREP TIME** 15 minutes **COOK TIME** 15 minutes

Bulgur is cracked whole-grain wheat that has a deep, nutty flavor. It's a staple in many Middle Eastern and Mediterranean dishes and has a texture similar to quinoa or couscous. Bulgur is easy to make and extremely versatile.

3 cups water

1 cup bulgur

1 (9-ounce) package cooked lentils

1 cup halved cherry tomatoes

¼ cup minced scallions

¼ cup sliced kalamata olives

1 cup chopped fresh parsley

2 teaspoons ground cumin

Juice of 1 lemon

2 tablespoons extra-virgin olive oil

1 tablespoon red wine vinegar

¼ teaspoon sea salt

1. In a small saucepan, bring the water to a boil over medium heat. Add the bulgur, cover, reduce the heat, and simmer for 12 minutes, or until the bulgur is tender. Set aside to cool.

2. In a large bowl, combine the lentils, tomatoes, scallions, olives, parsley, and cumin and toss well.

3. In a small bowl, whisk together the lemon juice, olive oil, vinegar, and salt. Add the dressing to the lentil mixture and toss to combine well.

4. Add the cooled bulgur to the lentils and mix well.

INGREDIENT TIP: *Another way to cook the bulgur is to place it in a heatproof dish and pour in enough boiling water to cover. Stir well, cover the dish, and let it sit for 30 minutes.*

PER SERVING: Calories: 284; Protein: 11g; Carbohydrates: 44g; Fiber: 11g; Total fat: 9g; Saturated fat: 1g; Sugar: 3g; Sodium: 160mg

PASTA E FAGIOLI SOUP

SERVES 6   **PREP TIME** 10 minutes   **COOK TIME** 20 minutes

The name of this traditional Italian soup means "pasta and beans." This is a dish that reminds me of my childhood. It's a comfort food my mother made often; it's quick, easy, and nourishing. Serve this dish with a side salad or a hearty piece of whole-grain bread.

2 tablespoons extra-virgin olive oil

1 medium yellow onion, finely chopped

1 cup diced carrot

1 cup diced celery

4 garlic cloves, minced

1 cup ditalini pasta

4 cups low-sodium vegetable stock

2 cups water

1 (15-ounce) can low-sodium tomato sauce

1 (15-ounce) can no-salt-added diced tomatoes, with their juices

½ teaspoon sea salt

Freshly ground black pepper

2 (15-ounce) cans low-sodium cannellini beans, drained and rinsed

1. In a large soup pot or Dutch oven, heat the oil over medium heat. Add the onion, carrot, and celery and sauté for 8 to 10 minutes, until the onion is translucent and the carrot and celery are soft. Add the garlic and stir for 1 minute, or until fragrant.

2. Add the pasta, stock, water, tomato sauce, diced tomatoes and their juices, salt, pepper, and beans. Bring to a boil and stir to combine. Cook uncovered for 10 minutes, or until the pasta is tender.

VARIATION: *You can also use elbow pasta in this recipe. Or to make this recipe gluten-free and higher in protein and nutrients, use chickpea or lentil pasta.*

PER SERVING: Calories: 278; Protein: 12g; Carbohydrates: 45g; Fiber: 11g; Total fat: 5g; Saturated fat: 1g; Sugar: 7g; Sodium: 254mg

LENTIL-BARLEY SOUP

SERVES 6   **PREP TIME** 10 minutes   **COOK TIME** 45 minutes

Lentils are a budget-friendly, nutrient-dense food packed with iron, phyto-chemicals, and fiber. Combining lentils with barley creates a nutrition powerhouse dish with additional B vitamins, magnesium, manganese, and selenium. Barley also contains antioxidants, including some lutein and zea-xanthin, which help protect against free radicals, especially in the eyes.

2 tablespoons extra-virgin olive oil

1 yellow onion, diced

2 carrots, peeled and diced

2 celery stalks, diced

4 garlic cloves

1 cup red lentils, rinsed

½ cup pearled barley

4 cups low-sodium vegetable stock

4 cups water

¾ teaspoon sea salt

1 teaspoon ground cumin

3 cups chopped stemmed kale

1. In a large soup pot or Dutch oven, heat the olive oil over medium heat. Add the onion, carrot, and celery and sauté for 3 minutes, or until the onion is translucent. Stir in the garlic for 1 minute, or until fragrant.

2. Add the lentils, barley, stock, water, salt, and cumin. Bring to a boil, then reduce the heat, cover, and simmer for 30 minutes, or until the lentils and barley are tender.

3. Add the kale and stir until wilted.

VARIATION: *You can use yellow (golden) or green lentils in place of red lentils or try a mix of colors.*

PER SERVING: Calories: 238; Protein: 10g; Carbohydrates: 38g; Fiber: 7g; Total fat: 6g; Saturated fat: 1g; Sugar: 2g; Sodium: 262mg

SPLIT PEA AND CARROT SOUP

SERVES 6 **PREP TIME** 15 minutes **COOK TIME** 1 hour 45 minutes

This soup takes a bit longer to make, but after all of the ingredients are simmering in the pot, it's all hands-off time. I tend to make this soup on the weekend, leaving it to cook while I relax nearby with a good book. This hearty one-pot dish makes a great Sunday dinner, and the leftovers are perfect for lunches. Enjoy with a slice of whole-grain bread.

2 tablespoons extra-virgin olive oil

1 yellow onion, diced

3 medium carrots, peeled and diced

2 celery stalks, diced

2 garlic cloves, minced

¼ teaspoon ground cumin

2 Yukon Gold potatoes, peeled and diced

2 cups green split peas

4 cups low-sodium vegetable stock

4 cups water

½ teaspoon sea salt

⅛ teaspoon freshly ground black pepper

1. In a large soup pot or Dutch oven, heat the oil over medium heat. Add the onion, carrot, and celery and sauté for 10 minutes, or until the vegetables are soft and the onion is translucent. Add the garlic and cumin and stir for 1 minute, or until fragrant.

2. Add the potatoes, split peas, stock, water, salt, and pepper. Bring to a boil, then reduce the heat and simmer, uncovered, for 1 hour 30 minutes, stirring occasionally, until the split peas are tender.

LEFTOVERS TIP: *Double this recipe and store leftovers in an airtight container for up to 1 week in the refrigerator or up to 3 months in the freezer. When reheating, add a little vegetable stock or water if the soup has thickened while sitting.*

PER SERVING: Calories: 388; Protein: 19g; Carbohydrates: 69g; Fiber: 21g; Total fat: 6g; Saturated fat: 1g; Sugar: 9g; Sodium: 141mg

MANGO-GINGER RICE BOWLS

SERVES 4   **PREP TIME** 10 minutes   **COOK TIME** 10 minutes

Mango and ginger are a combo you will begin to crave. Add black beans with a squeeze of lime juice, and you'll be obsessed! Mangos are in season from spring to summer, but frozen mangos work well in this recipe, too. Try topping this dish with some sesame seeds and chopped fresh cilantro.

4 cups frozen cooked
brown rice

2 tablespoons water

1 (15-ounce) can
low-sodium black beans,
drained and rinsed

1 cup fresh or frozen
(thawed) mango
cubes (½-inch)

1 cup shredded
red cabbage

1 cucumber, cut into
½-inch cubes

2 avocados, peeled,
pitted, and cut into
½-inch cubes

Juice of 1 lime

2 tablespoons honey

1 teaspoon minced
fresh ginger

¼ teaspoon sea salt

½ cup Carrot-Ginger
Dressing (page 131)

1. In a medium skillet, combine the rice and water and cook for 7 minutes, or until heated through.

2. Meanwhile, in a large bowl, mix together the black beans, mango, cabbage, cucumber, avocado, lime juice, honey, ginger, and salt.

3. Divide the rice among four bowls. Dividing evenly, top with the mango and bean mixture. Drizzle 2 tablespoons dressing over each bowl and serve.

INGREDIENT TIP: *When buying a mango in season, squeeze the mango gently. A ripe mango will give slightly. There may also be a slight fruity aroma by the stem. Do not focus on color; it is not an indicator of ripeness.*

....

PER SERVING: Calories: 636; Protein: 14g; Carbohydrates: 96g; Fiber: 18g; Total fat: 25g; Saturated fat: 4g; Sugar: 23g; Sodium: 210mg

BEET POKE BOWLS

30
GF

SERVES 4   **PREP TIME** 15 minutes   **COOK TIME** 5 minutes

Poke is a Hawaiian dish of raw fish cut in chunks (poke means chunk in Hawaiian). Using cooked beets is a fun way to make this popular dish vegetarian. Balance your bowl with protein- and fiber-rich add-ins to keep you feeling satisfied.

2 tablespoons
coconut aminos

1 teaspoon minced
fresh ginger

2 (8-ounce) packages
cooked beets, cut into
1-inch cubes

4 cups frozen
cooked quinoa

1 cup frozen
shelled edamame

2 carrots, peeled
and julienned

2 avocados, peeled, pitted,
and cut into 1-inch cubes

4 tablespoons hemp hearts

½ cup Chipotle Tahini
Dressing (page 132)

1. In a large bowl, whisk together the coconut aminos and ginger. Add the beets and toss. Set aside.

2. In a microwave-safe bowl, microwave the frozen quinoa on high for 4 minutes, or until warmed through. (Or combine it in a small saucepan with ¼ cup water, cover, and warm over low heat for about 10 minutes.)

3. Divide the quinoa among four bowls. Dividing evenly, top each bowl with the edamame, carrots, and avocado. Mound the beets in the center of each bowl. Sprinkle 1 tablespoon hemp hearts and drizzle 2 tablespoons dressing over each.

VARIATION: *If you don't like spicy food, use the Green Tahini Sauce (page 127) or Carrot-Ginger Dressing (page 131) instead. To make this dish soy-free, switch out the edamame for the same quantity of rinsed canned low-sodium chickpeas.*

PER SERVING: Calories: 541; Protein: 18g; Carbohydrates: 71g; Fiber: 18g; Total fat: 23g; Saturated fat: 3g; Sugar: 16g; Sodium: 359mg

SPICY TOFU PEANUT BOWLS

SERVES 4   **PREP TIME** 15 minutes, plus 30 minutes to drain   **COOK TIME** 15 minutes

Made from condensed soy milk, tofu is a high-protein food that contains all nine essential amino acids. Choose organic tofu, when available, and if it fits in your budget, so you know it's made from non-GMO soybeans.

1 (14-ounce) package extra-firm tofu

4 cups frozen cooked brown rice

1 tablespoon sesame oil

4 scallions, diced, white and green parts kept separate

2 bell peppers (red and orange), diced

3 tablespoons 50% reduced-sodium tamari

1 tablespoon Thai red curry paste

1 tablespoon unseasoned rice vinegar

3 tablespoons no-added-sugar creamy peanut butter

1 cup water

1 (15-ounce) can low-sodium chickpeas, drained and rinsed

2 tablespoons chopped peanuts (optional)

Lime wedges, for serving (optional)

1. Drain the tofu and press it between two paper towels. Cut into 1-inch cubes.

2. Meanwhile, in a microwave-safe bowl, microwave the frozen brown rice on high for 4 minutes, or until warmed through. (Or combine it in a small saucepan with ¼ cup water, cover, and warm over low heat for about 10 minutes.)

3. Divide the rice among four bowls.

4. In a medium skillet, heat the sesame oil. Add the scallion whites and sauté for 2 minutes, or until they're tender. Add the tofu cubes and bell peppers and sauté for about 8 minutes, or until the tofu is brown on each side and the peppers are soft.

5. In a small bowl, whisk together the tamari, curry paste, vinegar, peanut butter, and water. Stir into the pan along with the chickpeas. Stir and heat through. Add water if needed.

6. Dividing evenly, top the rice with the tofu and chickpea mixture. Sprinkle with the scallion greens and optional toppings, if using.

PER SERVING: Calories: 552; Protein: 25g; Carbohydrates: 76g; Fiber: 12g; Total fat: 19g; Saturated fat: 2g; Sugar: 6g; Sodium: 324mg

ROOT VEGETABLE FARRO BOWLS WITH GREEN TAHINI SAUCE

DF

NF

SF

SERVES 6   **PREP TIME** 15 minutes   **COOK TIME** 40 minutes

Farro is a good source of protein, fiber, B vitamins, and iron. It's a better alternative to refined grains and has a nutty flavor and texture similar to barley. Farro is not gluten-free, though.

1 pound sweet potatoes, scrubbed and cut into ½-inch cubes

2 carrots, peeled and cut into ½-inch cubes

2 parsnips, peeled and cut into ½-inch cubes

2 beets, peeled and cut into ½-inch cubes

2 tablespoons extra-virgin olive oil

¼ teaspoon sea salt

⅛ teaspoon freshly ground black pepper

1 (15-ounce) can low-sodium chickpeas, drained and rinsed

4 cups low-sodium vegetable stock

2 cups water

1 cup semi-pearled farro, rinsed

½ cup Green Tahini Sauce (page 127)

1. Preheat the oven to 400°F. Line a rimmed baking sheet with unbleached parchment paper.

2. In a large bowl, toss together the sweet potatoes, carrots, parsnips, beets, olive oil, salt, and pepper. Spread on the prepared baking sheet.

3. Roast the vegetables for 20 minutes. Turn and roast for another 15 minutes, or until tender and slightly browned. Add the chickpeas to the roasted vegetables and roast for another 5 minutes.

4. Meanwhile, in a large soup pot or Dutch oven, bring the stock and water to a boil over high heat. Add the farro and return to a boil, then reduce the heat to medium and cook, uncovered, for 30 minutes, or until the farro is tender. Drain.

5. Divide the farro among four bowls. Dividing evenly, top with the vegetables and chickpeas. Drizzle 2 tablespoons tahini sauce over each bowl.

INGREDIENT TIP: *Look for semi-pearled farro. It is minimally processed to remove some of the bran but still retains its fiber and nutrients, making it a healthy whole-grain option with a shorter cooking time and a more tender bite than the unpearled variety.*

PER SERVING: Calories: 407; Protein: 9g; Carbohydrates: 67g; Fiber: 14g; Total fat: 13g; Saturated fat: 1g; Sugar: 13g; Sodium: 259mg

SMOKY THREE-BEAN CHILI

SERVES 4 **PREP TIME** 10 minutes **COOK TIME** 55 minutes

Chili can be the base for so many meals. This version can be added to tacos, spooned over a salad, or served with Cashew Queso (page 122). Make extras on the weekend and you can enjoy it all week.

1 tablespoon extra-virgin olive oil

1 yellow onion, diced

4 garlic cloves, minced

½ cup diced carrot

½ cup diced celery

3 tablespoons chili powder

2 teaspoons smoked paprika

¼ teaspoon sea salt

1 (28-ounce) can no-salt-added fired-roasted diced tomatoes, with their juices

1 cup low-sodium vegetable stock

3 cups water

1 (15-ounce) can low-sodium great northern beans, drained and rinsed

1 (15-ounce) can low-sodium red kidney beans, drained and rinsed

1 (15-ounce) can low-sodium black beans, drained and rinsed

1. In a large soup pot or Dutch oven, heat the olive oil over medium heat. Add the onion and garlic and sauté for 3 minutes, or until the onion is translucent. Add the carrot and celery and sauté for 5 minutes. Add the chili powder, smoked paprika, and salt and stir together until the spices are fragrant.

2. Add the diced tomatoes and juices, vegetable stock, water, and all the beans. Cover and cook on low for 45 minutes to meld the flavors.

VARIATION: *Serve with shredded cheese, sour cream, or Avocado Crema (page 129) on top. Or keep it vegan with crushed tortillas, chopped scallions, or sliced avocado.*

PER SERVING: Calories: 346; Protein: 20g; Carbohydrates: 59g; Fiber: 23g; Total fat: 6g; Saturated fat: 1g; Sugar: 9g; Sodium: 242mg

FARRO MUSHROOM CHILI

SERVES 6   **PREP TIME** 10 minutes   **COOK TIME** 40 minutes

Farro is packed with protein, B vitamins, and iron—making it a great fit for a vegetarian lifestyle. Farro takes on the flavors you cook it with, so it's extremely versatile. It's a hearty grain with a tender bite and it doesn't get soggy, making it the perfect addition to soup or chili.

1 tablespoon extra-virgin olive oil

1 yellow onion, diced

4 garlic cloves, minced

2 large red bell peppers, diced

8 ounces white mushrooms, diced

2 tablespoons chili powder

½ teaspoon sea salt

1 (28-ounce) can no-salt-added diced tomatoes, with their juices

1 cup low-sodium vegetable stock

3 cups water

1 cup pearled farro

1 (29-ounce) can low-sodium black beans, drained and rinsed

½ cup frozen corn kernels

1. In a large soup pot or Dutch oven, heat the olive oil over medium heat. Add the onion and garlic and sauté for about 3 minutes, or until the onion is translucent.

2. Add the bell peppers and mushrooms and sauté for 5 minutes. Add the chili powder and salt and stir until the spices are fragrant.

3. Add the diced tomatoes and their juices vegetable stock, water, farro, black beans, and corn. Cover and cook over low heat for 30 minutes.

VARIATION: *Chili is the perfect dish to help cut down on food waste. Ten minutes before it's done, cube and add any vegetables in your fridge, cooked or raw, that would otherwise need to be tossed, such as zucchini, broccoli, and cauliflower.*

PER SERVING: Calories: 381; Protein: 19g; Carbohydrates: 71g; Fiber: 20g; Total fat: 5g; Saturated fat: 1g; Sugar: 8g; Sodium: 241mg

Skillet Pizza with Pumpkin Seed Pesto ▸ 82

CHAPTER 6

HEARTY ENTRÉES

TOFU NUGGETS WITH MAPLE-MUSTARD DIPPING SAUCE

SERVES 4   **PREP TIME** 15 minutes   **COOK TIME** 15 minutes

Tofu is a good source of plant-based protein and contains all nine essential amino acids, as well as iron, calcium, magnesium, zinc, and B vitamins. This kid-friendly dish makes a fabulous meatless meal the entire family will love.

1 (14-ounce) package extra-firm tofu

¼ cup almond flour

2 large eggs

½ cup whole wheat bread crumbs

2 tablespoons nutritional yeast

1 teaspoon onion powder

1 teaspoon garlic powder

½ teaspoon sea salt

¼ teaspoon freshly ground black pepper

1 tablespoon dried parsley

2 tablespoons extra-virgin olive oil

½ cup Maple-Mustard Dipping Sauce (page 128)

1. Drain the tofu and press it between two paper towels.

2. Set up a dredging station: Place the almond flour in a shallow bowl. Whisk the eggs in a small bowl. In a medium bowl, combine the bread crumbs, nutritional yeast, onion powder, garlic powder, salt, pepper, and parsley.

3. Once the tofu is pressed, slice the block lengthwise in quarters by slicing in half first, then slicing each half in half again. Next, cut each of the four layers in half lengthwise. Then cut each of those halves crosswise into quarters (pieces should be about 1 by 2 inches each). This will create 32 nuggets.

4. To assemble the nuggets, coat them first in the almond flour, then dip in the egg to evenly coat, and finally coat all sides in the bread crumb mixture. Place the coated nuggets on a large plate as you work.

5. In a medium skillet, heat the olive oil over medium heat. Working in two batches, add the breaded tofu nuggets in a single layer and cook for 2 to 3 minutes on each side, until browned all over.

6. Serve 8 nuggets per person, with the dipping sauce on the side.

INGREDIENT TIP: *Pressing the water out of tofu will improve its taste and texture. Even extra-firm tofu will benefit from a little pressing before cooking.*

....

PER SERVING: Calories: 285; Protein: 15g; Carbohydrates: 12g; Fiber: 2g; Total fat: 21g; Saturated fat: 2g; Sugar: 4g; Sodium: 314mg

SKILLET PIZZA WITH PUMPKIN SEED PESTO

SERVES 4 **PREP TIME** 15 minutes, plus 30 minutes to rise **COOK TIME** 30 minutes

Why order pizza from a restaurant when making your own at home can be so easy—and lots of fun? Pizza dough is readily available in grocery stores and can be frozen, so you always have a base for a pizza dinner on hand. But making your own dough can also be super easy, and a great activity for the entire family. Get everyone involved and customize the pizza by adding your favorite grilled veggies. You can also freeze this homemade version for up to 3 months.

FOR THE CRUST

1 (¼-ounce) envelope active dry yeast

1 cup warm (110°F) water

2 cups white whole wheat flour, plus more for dusting

1 teaspoon honey

½ teaspoon sea salt

2 tablespoons extra-virgin olive oil

Nonstick cooking spray

TO MAKE THE CRUST

1. In a medium bowl, dissolve the yeast in the warm water and let sit for 10 minutes.

2. In a large bowl, mix together the flour, yeast mixture, honey, salt, and olive oil and stir to form a dough. Dust a work surface with flour and knead the dough a few times. Form the dough into a ball, adding a bit more flour if the dough is too sticky. The dough should be only slightly sticky. Wipe out the bowl and mist with cooking spray. Return the dough to the bowl, cover loosely with a towel, and let the dough rise for 30 minutes.

3. Lay the dough out on the work surface and roll and pat into a round (don't worry about the final size yet). Mist a 12-inch oven-safe skillet (cast iron works great here) with cooking spray. Transfer the dough to the skillet and press it out to the edges of the skillet. Pinch all around the edges to make a ridge of crust.

4. Preheat the oven to 450°F.

2 tablespoons extra-virgin olive oil

¼ teaspoon sea salt

½ teaspoon garlic powder

1 small yellow squash, cut into ¼-inch-thick coins

1 small zucchini, cut into ¼-inch-thick coins

1 red bell pepper, cut into ½-inch-wide strips

½ red onion, sliced

Nonstick cooking spray

¼ cup Pumpkin Seed Pesto (page 123)

4 tablespoons part-skim ricotta cheese

TO MAKE THE TOPPINGS

5. While the dough rests, in a large bowl, whisk together the olive oil, salt, and garlic powder. Toss the squash, zucchini, bell pepper, and onion in the seasoned olive oil until the vegetables are well coated.

6. Mist a grill pan with cooking spray and heat over medium heat. Add the vegetables to the grill pan and cook on each side for 4 minutes. Set aside until you are ready to assemble the pizza.

TO FINISH THE PIZZA

7. Evenly spread the pesto all over the crust, then arrange the grilled vegetables on top. Add a 1-tablespoon dollop of ricotta cheese in each quarter of the dough.

8. Bake for 20 minutes, or until the crust is golden brown. Cut into 4 wedges to serve.

VARIATION: *Omit the ricotta cheese for a dairy-free version. If you miss that cheesy flavor, sprinkle on some nutritional yeast after the pizza comes out of the oven.*

PER SERVING: Calories: 413; Protein: 11g; Carbohydrates: 48g; Fiber: 5g; Total fat: 19g; Saturated fat: 3g; Sugar: 6g; Sodium: 185mg

SWEET POTATO AND CHICKPEA CURRY WITH SPINACH

SERVES 4 **PREP TIME** 10 minutes **COOK TIME** 30 minutes

Curry powder is a blend of spices that typically includes turmeric—a spice with the active compound curcumin, which is what gives curry its distinctive bold yellow color. Turmeric is also known for its anti-inflammatory properties, as well as being a potent antioxidant. A small amount of curry powder packs a lot of flavor into a variety of dishes and adds great nutrition, too. Enjoy this dish paired with your favorite whole grain, such as brown rice or whole wheat naan.

1 tablespoon extra-virgin olive oil

1 sweet onion, diced

3 garlic cloves, minced

1 pound sweet potatoes, peeled and cut into ½-inch cubes

1 (15-ounce) can low-sodium chickpeas, drained and rinsed

1 teaspoon ground cumin

1 teaspoon curry powder

½ teaspoon ground ginger

½ teaspoon ground turmeric

½ teaspoon sea salt

1 (14-ounce) can light coconut milk

2 tablespoons no-salt-added tomato paste

2 cups packed baby spinach

1. In a large soup pot or Dutch oven, heat the olive oil over medium heat. Add the onion and sauté for 5 minutes, or until translucent.

2. Add the garlic and sweet potatoes and sauté for 10 minutes, or until tender. Add the chickpeas, cumin, curry powder, ginger, turmeric, and salt and sauté until the spices are fragrant. Add the coconut milk and tomato paste, combine well, and simmer for 10 more minutes.

3. Add the spinach and stir for 1 or 2 minutes, until just wilted.

VARIATION: *Swap out the spinach and chickpeas here for whatever you have leftover from the previous week. Frozen vegetables would work well, too.*

PER SERVING: Calories: 328; Protein: 8g; Carbohydrates: 42g; Fiber: 8g; Total fat: 16g; Saturated fat: 10g; Sugar: 9g; Sodium: 350mg

BAKED PENNE WITH EGGPLANT RAGÙ

GF NF SF

SERVES 6   **PREP TIME** 10 minutes   **COOK TIME** 50 minutes

The rich texture of eggplant combined with tomatoes and melted mozzarella cheese is my kind of comfort food. I'll even chop up any vegetables I have on hand to sauté in place of the eggplant: Zucchini, yellow squash, asparagus, and butternut squash all work well.

1 (8-ounce) box lentil or chickpea penne pasta

1 tablespoon extra-virgin olive oil

1 small yellow onion, diced

1 eggplant, cut into 1-inch cubes

8 ounces baby bella mushrooms, diced

3 garlic cloves, minced

1 (28-ounce) can no-salt-added tomato puree

½ teaspoon sea salt

¼ teaspoon freshly ground black pepper

3 tablespoons chopped fresh basil, divided

1½ cups shredded part-skim mozzarella cheese

1. Preheat the oven to 350°F.

2. Fill a medium saucepan with water and bring to a boil. Add the pasta, stir, and cook for about 11 minutes, or according to the package instructions. Drain, rinse, and set aside.

3. Meanwhile, in a large oven-safe skillet, heat the olive oil over medium heat. Add the onion and sauté for 4 minutes. Add the eggplant, mushrooms, and garlic and sauté for 5 minutes to soften. Add the tomato puree, salt, pepper, and 1 tablespoon of basil. Stir the mixture well and bring to a boil. Reduce to a simmer, cover, and cook for 15 minutes to thicken and blend the flavors. Stir occasionally to prevent the sauce from sticking.

4. Add the cooked pasta to the skillet and combine well. Evenly spread the mozzarella on top and bake for 15 minutes. Top with the remaining basil and serve.

PER SERVING: Calories: 240; Protein: 10g; Carbohydrates: 36g; Fiber: 8g; Total fat: 8g; Saturated fat: 3g; Sugar: 8g; Sodium: 293mg

CHIPOTLE CAULIFLOWER-PISTACHIO TACOS

SERVES 6   **PREP TIME** 15 minutes   **COOK TIME** 25 minutes

Chipotle peppers impart a smoky, spicy flavor to many Mexican dishes. You can buy them dried, but, more commonly, they come in cans packed in adobo sauce.

2 tablespoons extra-virgin olive oil

1 sweet onion, chopped

3 garlic cloves, minced

2 carrots, grated

8 ounces baby bella mushrooms, thinly sliced

1 head cauliflower, cut into bite-size pieces

2 small canned chipotle peppers in adobo sauce, minced

¼ teaspoon sea salt

¼ teaspoon smoked paprika

1 teaspoon ground cumin

¼ cup chopped pistachios

1 (14.5-ounce) can no-salt-added fire-roasted diced tomatoes, drained

1 (15-ounce) can low-sodium black beans, drained and rinsed

12 (6-inch) corn tortillas

1 cup Avocado Crema (page 129)

3 tablespoons minced fresh cilantro

1. In a large soup pot or Dutch oven, heat the olive oil over medium heat. Add the onion and garlic and sauté for 4 minutes, or until the onion is translucent.

2. Add the carrot, mushrooms, and cauliflower and sauté for 10 minutes, or until tender. Stir in the chipotles, salt, smoked paprika, and cumin. Sauté for 1 minute, or until the spices are fragrant. Add the pistachios, tomatoes, and black beans. Reduce the heat and simmer for 10 minutes to heat through and thicken slightly.

3. A few at a time, wrap the tortillas in a damp paper towel and microwave for 30 seconds to warm them through.

4. Lay two warm tortillas on each of six plates. Dividing evenly, top the tortillas with the cauliflower-pistachio mixture. Drizzle each with Avocado Crema and sprinkle with cilantro, then fold the tortillas over to make tacos.

INGREDIENT TIP: *Once you open a can of chipotle peppers, mince the unsed ones and freeze them in small portions for future recipes.*

PER SERVING: Calories: 479; Protein: 18g; Carbohydrates: 74g; Fiber: 18g; Total fat: 16g; Saturated fat: 2g; Sugar: 11g; Sodium: 197mg

BLACK BEAN FALAFEL WITH CHIPOTLE TAHINI DRESSING

SERVES 4   **PREP TIME** 8 minutes   **COOK TIME** 22 minutes

Falafel is traditionally made with chickpeas or fava beans. I created this dish after I ran out of chickpeas one night and substituted black beans. Most recipes work with a number of different beans, so feel free to mix things up in all the bean recipes in this book. A variety of ingredients also ensures you get a variety of nutrients. Double this batch and enjoy the falafel in a whole-grain pita with greens, over a kale salad, or on top of a grain bowl.

1 (15-ounce) can low-sodium black beans, drained and rinsed

¼ cup pumpkin seeds

½ yellow onion, quartered

¼ cup fresh cilantro

¼ cup fresh parsley

4 garlic cloves, peeled

2 teaspoons ground cumin

¼ teaspoon sea salt

¼ cup old-fashioned rolled oats

Juice 1 lime

¼ cup Chipotle Tahini Dressing (page 132)

1. Preheat the oven to 375°F. Line a rimmed baking sheet with unbleached parchment paper.

2. In a food processor, combine the black beans, pumpkin seeds, onion, cilantro, parsley, garlic, cumin, salt, oats, and lime juice. Pulse several times to combine and create a coarse and chunky texture.

3. Use your hands to form the mixture into 1½-inch balls and place them on the sheet pan. Repeat with the remaining falafel mixture to make 12 balls.

4. Bake the falafel for 8 minutes. Flip the falafel and bake for 15 minutes longer, or until firm and set.

5. Serve drizzled with the dressing.

VARIATION: *To replace the fresh herbs with dried, use 2½ tablespoons dried parsley in place of fresh cilantro and fresh parsley. To replace the garlic cloves, use ½ teaspoon garlic powder.*

PER SERVING: Calories: 175; Protein: 9g; Carbohydrates: 24g; Fiber: 7g; Total fat: 5g; Saturated fat: 1g; Sugar: 2g; Sodium: 130mg

GARDEN BLACK BEAN BURGERS

SERVES 6   **PREP TIME** 10 minutes   **COOK TIME** 40 minutes

Making your own veggie burgers at home is healthy and budget-friendly.

1 tablespoon extra-virgin olive oil

1 yellow onion, chopped

2 garlic cloves, minced

4 ounces mushrooms, chopped

1 carrot, peeled and chopped

1 small head broccoli, chopped

1 teaspoon smoked paprika

½ teaspoon ground cumin

½ teaspoon sea salt

1 (15-ounce) can low-sodium black beans, drained and rinsed

¼ cup chopped pecans

2 tablespoons ground flaxseed

1 large egg

6 whole-grain burger buns

¼ cup Roasted Red Pepper and Walnut Sauce (page 126)

1. Preheat the oven to 350°F. Line a rimmed baking sheet with unbleached parchment paper.

2. In a medium skillet, heat the olive oil over medium heat. Add the onion and sauté for 4 minutes, or until translucent. Add the garlic, mushrooms, carrot, and broccoli and sauté for 10 minutes, or until the vegetables are tender. Add the smoked paprika, cumin, and salt and stir for 1 minute, or until the spices are fragrant.

3. Allow the vegetables to cool slightly, then transfer them to a food processor, along with the black beans, pecans, ground flaxseed, and egg. Pulse to combine, leaving the mixture a bit chunky.

4. Divide the burger mixture into 6 equal portions (about 3 tablespoons per portion). Roll each portion into a ball, then flatten it on the prepared baking sheet.

5. Bake for 15 minutes, flip the burgers, and bake on the other side for 10 minutes.

6. Serve each burger on a whole-grain bun, drizzled with the red pepper and walnut sauce.

....

PER SERVING: Calories: 284; Protein: 12g; Carbohydrates: 40g; Fiber: 8g; Total fat: 9g; Saturated fat: 1g; Sugar: 5g; Sodium: 344mg

BROCCOLI AND CHICKPEA STIR-FRY WITH CASHEWS

SERVES 4   **PREP TIME** 10 minutes   **COOK TIME** 20 minutes

Stir-fries are a quick and simple way to enjoy a variety of veggies. Keep your freezer stocked with frozen vegetables and cooked whole grains, and you can make meals like this in a flash. Pair this vegan stir-fry with a higher-protein grain such as sorghum, quinoa, or amaranth.

1 tablespoon extra-virgin olive oil

3 garlic cloves, minced, divided

2 heads broccoli, cut into bite-size pieces

1 red bell pepper, diced

4 ounces mushrooms, sliced

1 cup snow peas, trimmed

1 (15-ounce) can low-sodium chickpeas, drained and rinsed

½ cup cashews

3 tablespoons 50% reduced-sodium tamari

1 tablespoon pure maple syrup

1. In a large skillet or wok, heat the olive oil over medium-high heat. Add two-thirds of the minced garlic and sauté for 1 minute, or until fragrant.

2. Add the broccoli, bell pepper, mushrooms, and snow peas and sauté for 10 minutes, or until the vegetables are tender. Add the chickpeas and cashews and sauté for 5 minutes to heat through.

3. In a small bowl, whisk together the tamari, maple syrup, and remaining minced garlic. Pour over the vegetables and sauté for 3 minutes. Serve immediately.

VARIATION: *You can use honey instead of maple syrup. However, honey is not vegan. If that's an issue for you, but you want a more neutral flavor than maple, try using the same amount of agave syrup.*

PER SERVING: Calories: 275; Protein: 13g; Carbohydrates: 35g; Fiber: 9g; Total fat: 14g; Saturated fat: 2g; Sugar: 11g; Sodium: 354mg

PINTO BEAN AND VEGETABLE ENCHILADAS

SERVES 4   **PREP TIME** 15 minutes   **COOK TIME** 30 minutes

This is an easy, go-to meal that satisfies my entire family. I put some arugula on each plate and top it with two of these enchiladas and some sliced avocado or brown rice.

Nonstick cooking spray

2 tablespoons extra-virgin olive oil, divided

1 yellow onion, diced

1 yellow squash, chopped

1 red bell pepper, diced

1 cup frozen corn kernels

2 (15-ounce) cans low-sodium pinto beans, drained and rinsed

1 (4.5-ounce) can green chiles

1 cup low-sodium red enchilada sauce, divided

8 (6-inch) corn tortillas

1½ cups shredded reduced-fat (2%) mild cheddar cheese, divided

1 bunch scallions, chopped

1. Preheat the oven to 400°F. Mist a 9-by-13-inch baking dish with cooking spray.

2. In a medium skillet, heat 1 tablespoon of olive oil over medium heat. Add the onion and sauté for 4 minutes, or until translucent. Add the yellow squash, bell pepper, and corn and sauté for 8 minutes, until tender. Mix in the pinto beans and green chiles and cook for 3 minutes more to meld the flavors.

3. Pour one-third of the enchilada sauce evenly in the prepared baking dish.

4. Lay out the corn tortillas on a cutting board. Divide the vegetable-bean mixture evenly among the tortillas. Sprinkle the cheddar evenly on top. Spoon a generous 1½ teaspoons enchilada sauce on each. Roll up the tortillas and place them seam-side down in the baking dish.

5. Pour the remaining enchilada sauce over the tortillas and top with the remaining ¾ cup of cheddar and the scallions.

6. Cover the dish with aluminum foil and bake for 15 minutes, or until the cheese is melted.

....

PER SERVING (2 ENCHILADAS): Calories: 520; Protein: 28g; Carbohydrates: 79g; Fiber: 18g; Total fat: 12g; Saturated fat: 4g; Sugar: 7g; Sodium: 402mg

MUSHROOM AND ASPARAGUS RISOTTO

GF

NF

SF

SERVES 4   **PREP TIME** 10 minutes   **COOK TIME** 25 minutes

Risotto can be enjoyed as a hearty dish on its own or as a side dish with Grilled Vegetable and Portobello Skewers (page 98). For this recipe, I used chickpea rice because it's quick to make and adds creaminess, but you can substitute instant brown rice.

4 cups low-sodium vegetable stock

2 tablespoons extra-virgin olive oil, divided

2 shallots, finely diced

2 garlic cloves, minced

8 ounces baby bella mushrooms, sliced

1 bunch thin asparagus, trimmed and cut into 2-inch pieces

1 tablespoon unsalted butter

1½ cups chickpea rice

½ teaspoon sea salt

⅛ teaspoon freshly ground black pepper

¼ cup grated vegetarian parmesan cheese (optional)

2 tablespoons chopped fresh parsley (optional)

1. In a small saucepan, heat the vegetable stock over low heat. Cover and keep warm.

2. In a soup pot or Dutch oven, heat 1 tablespoon of olive oil over medium heat. Add the shallots and sauté for 3 minutes, or until softened and lightly browned. Add the garlic, mushrooms, and asparagus and sauté for 6 minutes, or until tender. Use a slotted spoon to transfer the vegetables to a bowl.

3. Set the same pot over medium heat and add the remaining 1 tablespoon of olive oil and the butter. When the butter melts, add the chickpea rice, salt, and pepper. Cook and stir the rice for 4 minutes. Start adding the warm vegetable stock 1 cup at a time, stirring the rice and cooking until almost all the stock is evaporated before adding another cup. In about 10 minutes the risotto should be creamy.

4. Stir in the cooked vegetables. If desired, stir in the parmesan, parsley, or both.

INGREDIENT TIP: *Most grocery stores carry chickpea rice or a blend that includes lentils as well.*

PER SERVING: Calories: 306; Protein: 12g; Carbohydrates: 38g; Fiber: 8g; Total fat: 13g; Saturated fat: 3g; Sugar: 8g; Sodium: 164mg

CREAMY MASHED POTATOES WITH LENTILS AND MUSHROOMS

SERVES 4   **PREP TIME** 10 minutes   **COOK TIME** 15 minutes

Potatoes are a good source of potassium and vitamin C, plus folate and vitamin B6. The combination of the olive oil, lentils, and nutritional yeast create a creamy texture and a flavor you'll soon be craving.

2 pounds Yukon Gold potatoes, peeled and cut into 2-inch cubes

3 tablespoons extra-virgin olive oil, divided

½ yellow onion, diced

3 garlic cloves, minced

8 ounces white mushrooms, diced

3 medium carrots, peeled and diced

2 celery stalks, diced

½ teaspoon sea salt, divided

2 (9-ounce) packages cooked lentils

1 tablespoon nutritional yeast

1. Put the potatoes in a medium saucepan and pour in enough water to cover. Cover and bring to a boil over high heat, then uncover, reduce the heat to medium, and cook for 15 minutes, or until tender.

2. Meanwhile, in a large skillet, heat 1 tablespoon of olive oil over medium heat. Add the onion and sauté for 4 minutes, or until translucent. Add the garlic, mushrooms, carrots, celery, and ¼ teaspoon of sea salt and sauté for 7 minutes, or until the vegetables are tender. Add the lentils and stir until they're warmed through.

3. When the potatoes are cooked, drain them and return to the saucepan. Mash them with a potato masher or an immersion blender. Add the remaining 2 tablespoons of olive oil, the nutritional yeast, and remaining ¼ teaspoon of salt and combine.

4. Mound the potatoes on each of four plates and top with lentils and vegetables.

PER SERVING: Calories: 454; Protein: 19g; Carbohydrates: 74g; Fiber: 17g; Total fat: 11g; Saturated fat: 2g; Sugar: 8g; Sodium: 204mg

BAKED SPAGHETTI SQUASH WITH EGGPLANT "MEATBALLS"

SERVES 4   **PREP TIME** 15 minutes   **COOK TIME** 45 minutes

The peak season for spaghetti squash is early fall through winter. It will stay fresh for up to 3 months stored in a cool and dry place, making it perfect to stock in your kitchen for a nutrient-packed dinner. Double the "meatballs" in this dish and freeze the leftovers for quick dinners later in the month.

DF
GF
NF
SF
V

2 tablespoons extra-virgin olive oil, divided

½ yellow onion, diced

3 garlic cloves, minced

1 small eggplant, peeled and cut into 1-inch cubes

4 ounces baby bella mushrooms, diced

2 medium spaghetti squash

⅛ teaspoon sea salt, plus ¼ teaspoon

1 (9-ounce) package cooked lentils

½ cup old-fashioned rolled oats

3 tablespoons dried parsley

1 (24-ounce) jar low-sodium, no-added-sugar tomato basil pasta sauce

1. Preheat the oven to 400°F. Line two rimmed baking sheets with unbleached parchment paper.

2. In a medium skillet, heat 1 tablespoon of olive oil over medium heat. Add the onion and sauté for 4 minutes, or until translucent. Add the garlic, eggplant, and mushrooms and sauté for 8 minutes, or until the eggplant is tender. Set aside to cool slightly. Hold on to the skillet for warming the tomato sauce (no need to wash it).

3. Meanwhile, cut the spaghetti squash in half lengthwise and scoop out the seeds. Use a fork to pierce the skin all over on both halves. Drizzle the remaining 1 tablespoon of olive oil and ⅛ teaspoon of salt over the flesh of each half. Place the halves on one prepared baking sheet, cut-side down. Set the baking sheet aside for the moment.

4. In a food processor, combine the cooked eggplant mixture, lentils, oats, remaining ¼ teaspoon of salt, and the parsley. Pulse to combine but do not puree. Use your hands to form the mixture into 16, 1½-inch balls and place them on the other prepared baking sheet.

continues ▶

BAKED SPAGHETTI SQUASH WITH EGGPLANT "MEATBALLS"

continued ▶

5. Transfer both baking sheets to the oven and bake the meatballs for 25 minutes, or until set and firm. Bake the spaghetti squash for 30 minutes, or until fork-tender.

6. While everything is in the oven, warm the tomato sauce in the skillet.

7. When the "meatballs" are done, add them to the warm tomato sauce and cook for 5 minutes.

8. When the spaghetti squash is done, hold each squash half with a potholder and shred the flesh with a fork, leaving the strings within the squash half. Ladle some tomato sauce into each squash half and use the fork to combine it with the spaghetti strings. Divide the "meatballs" among the 4 squash halves. Ladle the remaining tomato sauce on top of the "meatballs."

INGREDIENT TIP: *To enhance texture and flavor, add some chopped fresh tomatoes and garnish with fresh cilantro.*

VARIATION: *For a cheesy version, sprinkle ¼ cup of shredded part-skim mozzarella cheese over the "meatballs" on each squash half. The residual heat will melt the cheese. Or you can place the cheese-topped squash halves back on the baking sheet (be sure to remove the parchment paper) and run them under the broiler for 1 minute, or until the cheese is melted and slightly browned on top.*

PER SERVING: Calories: 332; Protein: 20g; Carbohydrates: 50g; Fiber: 7g; Total fat: 8g; Saturated fat: 3g; Sugar: 3g; Sodium: 424mg

BUTTERNUT SQUASH LASAGNA

GF

NF

SF

SERVES 8   **PREP TIME** 15 minutes   **COOK TIME** 50 minutes

Butternut squash creates a delicious creaminess and blends beautifully with the ricotta.

2 tablespoons extra-virgin olive oil

½ sweet onion, finely chopped

1 garlic clove, minced

1 (20-ounce) package cubed butternut squash

8 ounces baby bella mushrooms, sliced

2 (24-ounce) jars low-sodium, no-added-sugar tomato basil pasta sauce

1 (8-ounce) box oven-ready lentil lasagna noodles

2 cups part-skim ricotta cheese

1 cup firmly packed baby spinach

1½ cups shredded part-skim mozzarella cheese

1. Preheat the oven to 400°F.

2. In a large skillet, heat the olive oil over medium heat. Add the onion, garlic, squash, and mushrooms and sauté for 10 minutes, until soft. Transfer the vegetables to a large bowl and mash with a potato masher or puree in a food processor.

3. Spread half of one jar of tomato sauce over the bottom of a 9-by-13-inch baking dish. Cover with one-third of the noodles. They will expand during cooking, so they do not need to overlap. Top evenly with half the vegetables, then half the ricotta, half the spinach, ½ cup of mozzarella, and the remaining half jar of tomato sauce. Top with another layer of noodles, followed by the remaining vegetables, then the remaining ricotta, the remaining spinach, and another ½ cup of mozzarella. Top with another half jar of tomato sauce. Top with a final layer of noodles and cover with the remaining sauce and mozzarella.

4. Cover the dish with aluminum foil and bake for 35 minutes. Uncover and bake for an additional 5 minutes, or until the cheese is melted.

PER SERVING: Calories: 413; Protein: 20g; Carbohydrates: 48g; Fiber: 6g; Total fat: 14g; Saturated fat: 7g; Sugar: 11g; Sodium: 294mg

BLACK BEAN FAJITA SKILLET WITH CASHEW QUESO

SERVES 4   **PREP TIME** 15 minutes   **COOK TIME** 15 minutes

This meal is made often in my house. I freeze sliced bell peppers and onions for easier prep, and I always have canned beans on hand. This dish works well over a variety of whole grains, such as brown rice, or added to a corn tortilla or on top of leafy greens.

2 tablespoons extra-virgin olive oil, divided

1 sweet onion, cut into ½-inch-thick slices

1 red bell pepper, cut into ½-inch-wide strips

1 yellow bell pepper, cut into ½-inch-wide strips

1 large sweet potato, scrubbed and cut into 1-inch cubes

2 portobello mushroom caps, cut into ½-inch-thick slices

2 teaspoons chili powder

1 teaspoon ground cumin

½ teaspoon sea salt

Juice of 1 lime

1 (15-ounce) can low-sodium black beans, drained and rinsed

2 avocados, peeled, pitted, and sliced

¼ cup Cashew Queso (page 122)

1. In a large skillet, heat 1 tablespoon of olive oil over medium heat. Add the onion and sauté for 4 minutes, until translucent.

2. Meanwhile, in a large bowl, toss together the bell peppers, sweet potato, mushrooms, chili powder, cumin, salt, remaining 1 tablespoon of olive oil, and lime juice.

3. Add the vegetables to the skillet with the onions and sauté for 8 minutes, or until the vegetables are tender. Stir in the black beans and heat to warm through.

4. Serve topped with avocado slices and Cashew Queso.

INGREDIENT TIP: *If beans upset your stomach, when shopping for canned beans, look for brands that include kombu seaweed. Kombu seaweed contains enzymes that help break down the gas-producing sugars in beans. This ingredient will help you tolerate the beans better without compromising the taste or nutrition.*

PER SERVING: Calories: 384; Protein: 11g; Carbohydrates: 41g; Fiber: 16g; Total fat: 22g; Saturated fat: 3g; Sugar: 6g; Sodium: 218mg

VEGGIE MAC AND CHEESE

SERVES 4   **PREP TIME** 10 minutes   **COOK TIME** 20 minutes

Who doesn't love mac and cheese? To make this classic dish healthier, simply choose a nutrient-dense pasta, such as whole wheat, lentil, or chickpea pasta, and add a few veggies to pack in the nutrition.

1 (8-ounce) box whole wheat elbow macaroni

1 tablespoon extra-virgin olive oil

½ yellow onion, diced

2 garlic cloves, minced

1 pint cherry tomatoes, quartered

1 cup frozen cauliflower rice

1 cup chopped broccoli

1½ cups shredded reduced-fat (2%) cheddar cheese, divided

½ teaspoon sea salt

2 tablespoons nutritional yeast

1 tablespoon Dijon mustard

1. Position the top oven rack near the broiler and preheat to broil.

2. In a large saucepan, cook the elbow macaroni according to the package directions. Reserving ¼ cup of pasta water, drain the pasta and rinse.

3. Meanwhile, in an oven-safe skillet, heat the olive oil over medium heat. Add the onion and sauté for 4 minutes, or until translucent. Add the garlic, tomatoes, cauliflower rice, and broccoli and sauté for 7 minutes, or until tender.

4. Add the cooked elbow macaroni and reserved ¼ cup pasta water to the vegetables and stir to combine. Add 1 cup of cheddar, the salt, nutritional yeast, and mustard and stir again.

5. Remove from the heat and sprinkle the remaining ½ cup of cheddar on top. Place the skillet under the broiler for 2 minutes, or until the cheese is melted and beginning to brown.

VARIATION: *To make this dish vegan, swap out the cheddar cheese for ¾ cup Cashew Queso (page 122).*

PER SERVING: Calories: 332; Protein: 20g; Carbohydrates: 50g; Fiber: 7g; Total fat: 8g; Saturated fat: 3g; Sugar: 3g; Sodium: 424mg

GRILLED VEGETABLE AND PORTOBELLO SKEWERS

SERVES 4　　**PREP TIME** 15 minutes　　**COOK TIME** 10 minutes

This dish works well when you're cooking for a crowd. Prepare the skewers the day before and store them, covered, in the refrigerator. Simply put them on the grill 15 minutes before you are ready to eat. Pair this dish with Bulgur and Lentil Salad (page 68), which can also be prepared the night before.

Nonstick cooking spray

¼ cup extra-virgin olive oil

3 tablespoons balsamic vinegar

½ teaspoon sea salt

½ teaspoon garlic powder

1 yellow squash, cut into 1-inch-thick pieces

1 zucchini, cut into 1-inch-thick pieces

2 red bell peppers, cut into 1-inch pieces

1 red onion, cut into 1-inch-thick slices

2 portobello mushroom caps, cut into 1-inch-thick slices

1. Preheat a grill to medium-high heat. Mist the grates with cooking spray. (Or heat a grill pan on the stovetop over high heat and mist with cooking spray.)

2. In a large bowl, whisk together the olive oil, balsamic vinegar, salt, and garlic powder. Add the squash, zucchini, bell peppers, onion, and portobellos. Toss to coat the vegetables.

3. Thread each of eight metal skewers with pieces of squash, zucchini, peppers, onions, and portobellos, alternating the vegetables.

4. Grill the skewers for 5 minutes. Turn the skewers and grill for 5 minutes longer, or until the vegetables are soft.

LEFTOVERS TIP: *Add leftover grilled vegetables to the Root Vegetable Farro Bowls with Green Tahini Sauce (page 75) or the Pinto Bean and Vegetable Enchiladas (page 90). Grilled vegetables also make a great lunch on top of salads or added to eggs for an easy breakfast.*

PER SERVING: Calories: 185; Protein: 3g; Carbohydrates: 13g; Fiber: 3g; Total fat: 14g; Saturated fat: 2g; Sugar: 8g; Sodium: 159mg

DESSERTS

TOASTED QUINOA ENERGY BITES

MAKES 12 bites   **PREP TIME** 5 minutes, plus 30 minutes to chill
COOK TIME 5 minutes

Dates are a great addition to no-bake desserts. They add delicious sweetness, are packed with fiber and essential nutrients, and help bind the oats and other ingredients into an easy-to-roll bite. Dates also work well in a variety of dishes as a natural sweetener.

¼ cup uncooked quinoa, rinsed

4 pitted dates

¼ cup almonds

½ cup no-added-sugar creamy peanut butter

2 tablespoons ground flaxseed

2 tablespoons unsweetened shredded coconut

1 teaspoon pure vanilla extract

½ cup old-fashioned rolled oats

1. In a dry skillet, toast the quinoa over medium heat, stirring occasionally, for 4 minutes, or until the quinoa starts to pop and brown. Set aside.

2. In a food processor, combine the dates, almonds, and peanut butter and pulse 2 or 3 times. Add the ground flaxseed, coconut, vanilla, and oats and pulse until well blended.

3. Transfer the mixture to a bowl, fold in the toasted quinoa, cover, and refrigerate for at least 30 minutes.

4. Divide the chilled mixture into 12 equal portions. Using wet hands, roll each portion into a firm 1-inch ball. If the mixture feels too dry, add water by wetting your hands and rolling firmly again.

LEFTOVERS TIP: *Store in a sealed container in the refrigerator for up to 1 week or in the freezer for up to 3 months. Enjoy as a quick breakfast or a post-workout snack.*

PER SERVING (1 BITE): Calories: 116; Protein: 5g; Carbohydrates: 11g; Fiber: 2g; Total fat: 6g; Saturated fat: 1g; Sugar: 3g; Sodium: 66mg

ALMOND CHERRY BITES

MAKES 12 bites   **PREP TIME** 10 minutes, plus 30 minutes to chill

I love cherries! They pack a lot of flavor, along with many nutrients. I always have dried cherries in my pantry to add to baked goods, along with frozen ones in my freezer to add to smoothies or oatmeal. Dried cherries, especially tart cherries, are packed with anthocyanins, a polyphenol that acts as an antioxidant in your body. Cherry polyphenols may help fight inflammation, as well as protect against heart disease.

½ cup old-fashioned rolled oats

2 tablespoons chia seeds

¼ cup chopped almonds

¼ cup no-added-sugar almond butter

2 tablespoons ground flaxseed

¼ cup unsweetened dried tart cherries

2 tablespoons honey

1 teaspoon pure vanilla extract

¼ cup dairy-free dark chocolate chips

1. In a large bowl, mix together the oats, chia seeds, almonds, almond butter, ground flaxseed, cherries, honey, vanilla, and chocolate chips. Cover the bowl and refrigerate for at least 30 minutes.

2. Divide the chilled mixture into 12 equal portions (about 1 tablespoon each). Roll each portion into a ball.

INGREDIENT TIP: *Store almond butter in the refrigerator to extend its shelf life and to prevent separation.*

LEFTOVERS TIP: *Store in a sealed container in the refrigerator for up to 1 week or in the freezer for up to 3 months.*

PER SERVING (1 BITE): Calories: 117; Protein: 3g; Carbohydrates: 12g; Fiber: 3g; Total fat: 7g; Saturated fat: 1g; Sugar: 6g; Sodium: 5mg

CHICKPEA COOKIE DOUGH

I may enjoy eating cookie dough more than the baked cookies themselves. Do you agree? But eating raw cookie dough with eggs and flour risks food poisoning. This is the treat for you—it's safe, tasty, gluten-free, and nutrient-packed! Serve this decadent dessert in bowls.

1 (15-ounce) can low-sodium chickpeas, drained and rinsed

¼ cup no-added-sugar almond butter

¼ cup old-fashioned rolled oats

3 tablespoons pure maple syrup

1 tablespoon pure vanilla extract

¼ teaspoon sea salt

½ cup dairy-free dark chocolate chips

In a food processor, combine the chickpeas, almond butter, oats, maple syrup, vanilla, and salt and pulse until smooth. Fold in the chocolate chips.

VARIATION: *To make the recipe nut-free, use sunflower seed butter instead of almond butter.*

PER SERVING: Calories: 198; Protein: 6g; Carbohydrates: 22g; Fiber: 5g; Total fat: 10g; Saturated fat: 2g; Sugar: 10g; Sodium: 136mg

CHAI CHIA PUDDING WITH RASPBERRIES AND WALNUTS

SERVES 6 **PREP TIME** 5 minutes **COOK TIME** 10 minutes

Craving something sweet? In just 15 minutes you can make a warm, mouth-watering treat that will satisfy your sweet tooth and keep you feeling full. You can even enjoy this dish for breakfast or as a midday snack; it's that good and that filling!

1 cup chia seeds

4 cups unsweetened vanilla almond milk

2 tablespoons chai spice blend

2 tablespoons pure maple syrup

1 tablespoon pure vanilla extract

1 cup raspberries

½ cup chopped walnuts

1. In a medium saucepan, stir together the chia seeds, almond milk, chai spice, maple syrup, and vanilla. Bring to a boil over medium-high heat, then reduce the heat to medium-low and simmer, stirring, for 5 minutes, or until the mixture begins to thicken.

2. Divide the pudding among six bowls and top with the raspberries and walnuts. Serve warm or chilled. Store leftovers in an airtight container in the refrigerator for up to 3 days.

TIME SAVER: *Combine the chia seeds, almond milk, chai spice, maple syrup, and vanilla in an airtight container and store in the refrigerator overnight. The chia will thicken without any cooking. In the morning, simply heat the pudding and add the berries and nuts or enjoy chilled.*

PER SERVING: Calories: 329; Protein: 12g; Carbohydrates: 30g; Fiber: 16g; Total fat: 19g; Saturated fat: 2g; Sugar: 9g; Sodium: 87mg

NUT AND FRUIT DARK CHOCOLATE BARK

SERVES 12   **PREP TIME** 10 minutes, plus 30 minutes to chill

Enjoying dark chocolate in small amounts regularly may help reduce your chances of developing heart disease. Dark chocolate that has a cacao content of 70% or higher has more of the antioxidants known as flavonoids. A higher content of cacao could be bitter, though, so some products with really dark chocolate add a lot of sugar. Remember to always read the label. Store any leftovers in an airtight container.

Nonstick cooking spray

6 ounces dairy-free dark chocolate (70% cacao), coarsely chopped

3 tablespoons unsweetened dried cherries, divided

3 tablespoons unsweetened dried blueberries, divided

3 tablespoons chopped macadamia nuts, divided

¼ teaspoon coarse sea salt (optional)

1. Line an 8-by-8-inch baking dish with unbleached parchment paper and mist the paper with cooking spray.

2. In a double boiler or in a metal bowl set over a saucepan of heated water, melt the chocolate, stirring until smooth. Stir in half the cherries, blueberries, and nuts.

3. Spread the chocolate into the prepared baking dish. Evenly top with the remaining cherries, blueberries, and nuts. Sprinkle with the salt, if desired.

4. Refrigerate for 30 minutes, or until firm. Break the bark into 12 pieces.

VARIATION: *Make this recipe nut-free by replacing the macadamia nuts with pumpkin seeds or hemp hearts.*

PER SERVING: Calories: 118; Protein: 1g; Carbohydrates: 11g; Fiber: 2g; Total fat: 8g; Saturated fat: 4g; Sugar: 7g; Sodium: 6mg

STRAWBERRY OAT SQUARES

DF GF SF V

MAKES 9 squares   **PREP TIME** 10 minutes   **COOK TIME** 30 minutes

Baked strawberries create a delicious, sweet flavor in these bars, so you can add less sweetener. Combining coconut with the berries provides a tropical flavor for an indulgent, fresh treat. Drizzle on a teaspoon of Cashew Cream (page 121) for added richness.

Nonstick cooking spray

1 cup old-fashioned rolled oats, divided

¾ cup super-fine almond flour

¼ teaspoon sea salt

3 tablespoons unsweetened applesauce

¼ cup pure maple syrup

¼ cup no-added-sugar almond butter

2 teaspoons pure vanilla extract

1 cup diced strawberries

1 tablespoon avocado oil

2 tablespoons unsweetened shredded coconut

1. Preheat the oven to 375°F. Mist an 8-by-8-inch baking dish with cooking spray.

2. In a large bowl, mix together ¾ cup of oats, the almond flour, salt, applesauce, maple syrup, almond butter, and vanilla. Pour the batter into the prepared baking dish and evenly scatter the strawberries on top.

3. In a small bowl, combine the remaining ¼ cup of oats, avocado oil, and shredded coconut. Sprinkle evenly on top of the berries.

4. Transfer to the oven and bake for 30 minutes, or until firm and lightly browned.

5. Let cool in the pan for 10 minutes, then cut into 9 squares.

INGREDIENT TIP: *Frozen strawberries can be used in place of fresh. Let them thaw completely and pat dry well with paper towels before adding them to the dish.*

PER SERVING (1 SQUARE): Calories: 164; Protein: 4g; Carbohydrates: 16g; Fiber: 3g; Total fat: 10g; Saturated fat: 1g; Sugar: 7g; Sodium: 37mg

OAT FIG SQUARES

MAKES 9 squares   **PREP TIME** 10 minutes   **COOK TIME** 40 minutes

Figs are incredibly versatile and add healthy sweetness to dishes. Dried figs store well, so keep them on hand for other recipes.

Nonstick cooking spray

6 ounces organic dried figs

½ teaspoon sea salt, divided

2 cups old-fashioned rolled oats

1 cup super-fine almond flour

½ teaspoon aluminum-free baking soda

3 tablespoons avocado oil

2 tablespoons honey

2 teaspoons pure vanilla extract

1 ripe medium banana, mashed

1 large egg

2 tablespoons unsweetened shredded coconut

1. Preheat the oven to 350°F. Line an 8-by-8-inch baking dish with unbleached parchment paper and mist the paper with nonstick cooking spray.

2. Put the figs and ¼ teaspoon of salt in a small saucepan and pour in enough water to cover. Bring to a boil, reduce the heat, and simmer for 15 minutes. Drain the figs, then transfer them to a food processor and pulse until they're pureed.

3. While the figs cook, in a large bowl, combine the oats, almond flour, baking soda, avocado oil, honey, vanilla, banana, egg, and remaining ¼ teaspoon of salt. Mix well.

4. Scrape half of the batter into the prepared baking dish and use a spatula to spread it evenly in the pan. Dollop the fig puree on top and spread evenly with a spatula. Top with the remaining batter and sprinkle the shredded coconut on top.

5. Transfer to the oven and bake for 25 minutes, or until set and lightly browned.

6. Let cool in the pan for 10 minutes, then cut into 9 squares.

INGREDIENT TIP: *Look for dried figs that are unsulfured and have no added sugar.*

....

PER SERVING (1 SQUARE): Calories: 241; Protein: 6g; Carbohydrates: 32g; Fiber: 5g; Total fat: 11g; Saturated fat: 2g; Sugar: 15g; Sodium: 144mg

APPLE-PEAR-WALNUT CRUMBLE

SERVES 8 **PREP TIME** 10 minutes **COOK TIME** 35 minutes

I often make this dish at the beginning of the week and enjoy it as a mid-afternoon treat for many days. This dish can be enjoyed as a dessert as well as a topping for waffles, crepes, pancakes, or oatmeal, or even added to the batter. Enjoy your favorite choice of apple or pear, or make it your own by substituting another in-season fruit.

Nonstick cooking spray

¾ cup old-fashioned rolled oats

2 teaspoons ground cinnamon, divided

1 tablespoon avocado oil

4 tablespoons pure maple syrup, divided

1 large apple, peeled, cored, and sliced

1 pear, cored and sliced

1 tablespoon cornstarch

¼ cup chopped walnuts

¼ cup unsweetened dried cranberries

¼ teaspoon ground nutmeg

1. Preheat the oven to 350°F. Mist an 8-by-8-inch pan with cooking spray.

2. In a medium bowl, combine the oats, 1 teaspoon of cinnamon, avocado oil, and 1 tablespoon of maple syrup. Set aside.

3. In a separate medium bowl, mix together the apple slices, pear slices, cornstarch, walnuts, cranberries, nutmeg, remaining 1 teaspoon of cinnamon, and remaining 3 tablespoons of maple syrup.

4. Evenly spread the apple and pear mixture in the prepared pan. Spread the oat crumble evenly on the top of the fruit.

5. Transfer to the oven and bake for 35 minutes, or until the top is lightly browned and the fruit is soft.

LEFTOVERS TIP: *Store leftovers in an airtight container in the refrigerator for up to 5 days. Reheat single-serving portions in the microwave.*

PER SERVING: Calories: 144; Protein: 3g; Carbohydrates: 24g; Fiber: 3g; Total fat: 5g; Saturated fat: 1g; Sugar: 11g; Sodium: 4mg

CHOCOLATE CHIP
SKILLET COOKIE

SERVES 12   **PREP TIME** 10 minutes   **COOK TIME** 20 minutes

When you crave a cookie, you should have one! This recipe uses nutrient-dense ingredients, so you can enjoy your cookie and know you're nourishing yourself, too. This recipe is meant to be shared and can be served family-style topped with some ice cream. You can bake this cookie in a cast-iron skillet, if you have one.

Nonstick cooking spray

1¼ cups super-fine almond flour

¼ teaspoon baking soda

½ teaspoon sea salt

3 tablespoons no-added-sugar almond butter

3 tablespoons honey

2 large eggs

1 teaspoon pure vanilla extract

¼ cup finely chopped walnuts

¼ cup dairy-free dark chocolate chips

1. Preheat the oven to 350°F. Mist a 12-inch oven-safe skillet with cooking spray.

2. In a large bowl, combine the almond flour, baking soda, and salt. Set aside.

3. In a medium bowl, mix together the almond butter, honey, eggs, and vanilla. Gradually add the flour mixture to the almond butter mixture while whisking. Fold in the walnuts and chocolate chips.

4. Spread the dough in the skillet, using a spatula to push it to the edges of the pan. Bake for 18 minutes, or until the edges are slightly golden brown.

5. Let cool for 10 minutes, then cut into 12 wedges.

VARIATION: *Make this recipe vegan by leaving out the eggs, using maple syrup instead of honey, and substituting 2 tablespoons flaxseed whisked with 6 tablespoons water.*

PER SERVING (1 WEDGE): Calories: 133; Protein: 4g; Carbohydrates: 9g; Fiber: 2g; Total fat: 10g; Saturated fat: 2g; Sugar: 6g; Sodium: 89mg

PEANUT BUTTER OATMEAL COOKIES

30
DF
GF
SF

MAKES 24 cookies   **PREP TIME** 10 minutes   **COOK TIME** 15 minutes

Peanut butter is an extremely versatile ingredient that I could not be without. I often add this plant-based protein to smoothies, baked goods, snacks, and even savory dinner recipes. In fact, all of the ingredients in this recipe are always stocked in my kitchen.

1 cup no-added-sugar creamy peanut butter

1 large egg

¼ cup honey

1 teaspoon ground cinnamon

1 teaspoon pure vanilla extract

2 cups old-fashioned rolled oats

½ teaspoon baking soda

¼ teaspoon sea salt

1. Preheat the oven to 350°F. Line a rimmed baking sheet with unbleached parchment paper.

2. In a large bowl, blend the peanut butter, egg, honey, cinnamon, and vanilla. Set aside.

3. In a separate large bowl, combine the oats, baking soda, and salt. Gradually mix the oat mixture into the peanut butter mixture until well combined.

4. Scoop 1½ tablespoons of dough onto the prepared baking sheet for each cookie, leaving a scant inch between cookies. Press down on each cookie with a fork.

5. Bake the cookies for 14 minutes, or until browned around the edges. Let them cool on the pan. Store in an airtight container at room temperature.

INGREDIENT TIP: *When shopping for peanut butter, read the labels carefully and look for a brand that has the fewest ingredients—ideally, nothing but roasted peanuts.*

PER SERVING (2 COOKIES): Calories: 217; Protein: 10g; Carbohydrates: 25g; Fiber: 3g; Total fat: 10g; Saturated fat: 2g; Sugar: 8g; Sodium: 214mg

RASPBERRY VEGAN CHEESECAKE CUPS

SERVES 12   **PREP TIME** 20 minutes   **COOK TIME** 30 minutes

Raspberries have a short shelf life, so be sure to enjoy them shortly after you buy them. Frozen raspberries can be used in this dish as well.

1¼ cups cashews

1 cup pitted dates

1 cup pecans

¼ teaspoon sea salt

4 ounces silken tofu

Juice of 1 lemon

1 cup unsweetened cashew milk yogurt (or other plant-based yogurt)

¼ cup pure maple syrup, plus 1 tablespoon

2 teaspoons pure vanilla extract

¾ cup fresh raspberries

1. Preheat the oven to 350°F. Line 12 cups of a muffin tin with paper liners.

2. Put the cashews in a small saucepan and pour in enough water to cover. Bring to a boil, then reduce the heat and simmer for 20 minutes to soften. Drain.

3. Meanwhile, in a food processor, combine the dates, pecans, and salt and pulse until a crumble forms. Spoon 1 tablespoon of the pecan mixture into each muffin cup and press into the bottom. Set aside.

4. Clean the bowl of the food processor, then add the drained cashews, tofu, lemon juice, yogurt, ¼ cup of maple syrup, and the vanilla. Pulse until smooth. Evenly divide the filling among the cups.

5. Transfer to the oven and bake for 30 minutes.

6. Meanwhile, in a small saucepan, combine the raspberries and remaining 1 tablespoon of maple syrup. Heat the mixture over medium-low heat for 5 minutes. Set aside.

7. Let the cheesecakes cool in the pan. When they have cooled, carefully peel off the paper liners. Serve topped with 1 tablespoon of the raspberry sauce.

PER SERVING: Calories: 221; Protein: 5g; Carbohydrates: 24g; Fiber: 3g; Total fat: 13g; Saturated fat: 2g; Sugar: 16g; Sodium: 32mg

CHOCOLATE AVOCADO BROWNIES

MAKES 9 brownies   **PREP TIME** 10 minutes   **COOK TIME** 30 minutes

Avocado creates a moist texture in baked goods, and works as a vegan substitute for eggs and butter. This rich fruit also boosts the nutrition in a dessert: Just one-third of a medium avocado is packed with a full day's supply of 20 vitamins, minerals, and phytonutrients!

1 cup white whole
  wheat flour

½ cup unsweetened
  cocoa powder

¼ teaspoon baking soda

½ teaspoon sea salt

1 avocado, peeled
  and pitted

1 ripe banana, mashed

¼ cup pure maple syrup

2 teaspoons pure
  vanilla extract

2 large eggs

¼ cup dairy-free dark
  chocolate chips

¼ cup finely
  chopped walnuts

1. Preheat the oven to 350°F. Line an 8-by-8-inch baking dish with parchment paper.

2. In a large bowl, combine the flour, cocoa powder, baking soda, and salt. Set aside.

3. Scoop the avocado flesh into a medium bowl. Add the banana, maple syrup, and vanilla and mash together. Add the eggs one at a time, stirring until well combined after each addition. Gradually stir in the flour mixture until no streaks of flour remain. Fold in the chocolate chips and walnuts. Evenly spread the batter in the prepared baking dish.

4. Transfer to the oven and bake for 30 minutes, or until a toothpick inserted in the center comes out clean.

5. Let cool for 10 minutes in the pan before cutting into 9 brownies.

....

PER SERVING (1 BROWNIE): Calories: 200; Protein: 5g; Carbohydrates: 27g; Fiber: 4g; Total fat: 9g; Saturated fat: 3g; Sugar: 9g; Sodium: 122mg

CARROT CAKE MUFFINS

MAKES 12 muffins **PREP TIME** 15 minutes **COOK TIME** 20 minutes

I cannot resist carrot cake, especially when it's made into a grab-and-go muffin. These muffins are super moist and not too sweet. Enjoy one as a snack or as a breakfast with Greek yogurt. If you love frosting, try it topped with Cashew Cream (page 121) or drizzle with the lemon glaze from Maine Potato-Blueberry Doughnuts (page 115).

Nonstick cooking spray

1½ cups white whole wheat flour

1½ teaspoons baking soda

2 teaspoons ground cinnamon

¼ teaspoon ground nutmeg

¼ teaspoon sea salt

1 cup finely shredded carrots

¼ cup golden raisins

¼ cup chopped pecans

2 tablespoons avocado oil

¼ cup pure maple syrup

½ cup unsweetened applesauce

2 large eggs

1 teaspoon pure vanilla extract

1. Preheat the oven to 350°F. Mist 12 cups of a muffin tin with cooking spray.

2. In a large bowl, combine the flour, baking soda, cinnamon, nutmeg, and salt.

3. In a separate large bowl, combine the shredded carrots, raisins, pecans, oil, maple syrup, applesauce, eggs, and vanilla. Gradually add the flour mixture to the carrot mixture and combine well.

4. Divide the batter among the prepared muffin cups, filling them about three-quarters full.

5. Transfer to the oven and bake for 20 minutes, or until a toothpick inserted in the center of a muffin comes out clean.

6. Let the muffins cool in the pan.

VARIATION: *Make this recipe vegan by swapping out the 2 eggs for 3 tablespoons flaxseed whisked with 6 tablespoons water.*

PER SERVING (1 MUFFIN): Calories: 143; Protein: 3g; Carbohydrates: 22g; Fiber: 1g; Total fat: 5g; Saturated fat: 1g; Sugar: 7g; Sodium: 203mg

MAINE POTATO-BLUEBERRY DOUGHNUTS WITH LEMON GLAZE

DF

GF

SF

MAKES 6 doughnuts   **PREP TIME** 10 minutes   **COOK TIME** 30 minutes

After trying my first potato doughnut while vacationing in Maine, I was determined to re-create them at home. Adding potato to the mix creates a creamy smoothness without altering the taste, and packs in vitamin C, B vitamins, and fiber. Try to find wild blueberries, if possible, because they are higher in anthocyanins and antioxidants than farmed blueberries.

FOR THE DOUGHNUTS

Nonstick cooking spray

1 small russet potato, peeled and cut into 2-inch cubes

1 large egg

¼ cup pure maple syrup

½ cup unsweetened applesauce

2 tablespoons avocado oil

1 teaspoon pure vanilla extract

2 cups super-fine almond flour

2 teaspoons aluminum-free baking powder

¼ teaspoon sea salt

¼ cup frozen wild blueberries, thawed

TO MAKE THE DOUGHNUTS

1. Preheat the oven to 375°F. Mist a 6-count doughnut pan with cooking spray.

2. Put the potato in a small saucepan and pour in enough water to cover. Bring to a boil over high heat, reduce the heat to medium, and cook for 10 minutes, or until tender. Drain.

3. In a large bowl, mash together the cooked potatoes, egg, maple syrup, applesauce, avocado oil, and vanilla.

4. In a separate large bowl, combine the almond flour, baking powder, and salt. Gradually stir the almond flour mixture into the potato mixture until well combined. Carefully fold in the blueberries. Fill each doughnut cavity with the batter.

5. Transfer the pan to the oven and bake the doughnuts for 12 minutes, or until golden brown.

continues ▶

MAINE POTATO-BLUEBERRY DOUGHNUTS WITH LEMON GLAZE

continued ▶

FOR THE GLAZE

3 tablespoons
confectioners' sugar

1 tablespoon fresh
lemon juice

2 teaspoons unsweetened
vanilla almond milk

TO MAKE THE GLAZE

6. While the doughnuts are baking, in a small bowl, whisk together the sugar, lemon juice, and almond milk.

7. Cool the doughnuts in the pan on a rack for 10 minutes. Then evenly drizzle the lemon glaze over each doughnut.

INGREDIENT TIP: *Wild blueberries are available year-round in the freezer section. Fresh blueberries, or other berries, can also be used.*

VARIATION: *If you don't have a doughnut pan, make 6 muffins instead. Just follow the recipe as written.*

PER SERVING (1 DOUGHNUT): Calories: 247; Protein: 6g; Carbohydrates: 24g; Fiber: 3g; Total fat: 15g; Saturated fat: 2g; Sugar: 14g; Sodium: 229mg

Pumpkin Seed Pesto ▸ *123*

CHAPTER 8

STAPLES, SAUCES, AND DRESSINGS

VEGETABLE MARINADE

MAKES 1 cup **PREP TIME** 5 minutes

When you marinate raw vegetables, you tenderize them and infuse them with herbs and other great flavors. Check out the Chopped Raw Salad (page 66) for an idea of proportion of vegetables to marinade.

2 garlic cloves,
   coarsely chopped

½ cup red wine vinegar

1 tablespoon Dijon mustard

Juice of 1 lemon

½ teaspoon sea salt

⅛ teaspoon freshly ground
   black pepper

½ cup extra-virgin olive oil

In a food processor or high-powered blender, combine the garlic, vinegar, mustard, lemon juice, salt, and pepper. With the machine running, gradually add the olive oil and continue to blend until the marinade is smooth. Transfer to an airtight container and store in the refrigerator for up to 7 days.

VARIATION: *For a sweeter marinade, add 3 tablespoons agave nectar while blending.*

PER SERVING (2 TABLESPOONS): Calories: 126; Protein: 0g; Carbohydrates: 1g; Fiber: 0g; Total fat: 14g; Saturated fat: 2g; Sugar: 0g; Sodium: 96mg

CASHEW CREAM

MAKES 2 cups   **PREP TIME** 5 minutes, plus overnight to soak

I have a sweet tooth. This cream topping satisfies my cravings without any processed sugars. To create the cream-like texture, it's best to soak the cashews in water overnight. Try it as a topping on Berry Chia Overnight Oats (page 37), Baked Cherry Oatmeal (page 38), or Blueberry and Banana French Toast Bake (page 42).

2 cups raw cashews

1 cup unsweetened vanilla oat milk

¼ cup pure maple syrup

2 teaspoons pure vanilla extract

3 tablespoons avocado oil

1½ teaspoons ground cinnamon

¼ teaspoon sea salt

1. Put the cashews in a medium bowl and cover with cold water. Cover the bowl and soak overnight.

2. Drain the soaked cashews and add them to a food processor or high-powered blender along with the oat milk, maple syrup, vanilla, avocado oil, cinnamon, and salt. Blend until creamy and smooth.

INGREDIENT TIP: *If you are short on time, combine the cashews in a saucepan with water to cover. Bring to a boil. Remove from the heat, cover, and let sit for 1 hour, or until the cashews are softened.*

PER SERVING (2 TABLESPOONS): Calories: 139; Protein: 4g; Carbohydrates: 9g; Fiber: 1g; Total fat: 10g; Saturated fat: 2g; Sugar: 4g; Sodium: 20mg

CASHEW QUESO

MAKES 2 cups   **PREP TIME** 5 minutes, plus overnight to soak

This cashew cream is a creamy, nondairy alternative to cheese sauce. The cashews, combined with the nutritional yeast, create a smooth texture with a nutty, cheesy taste. It's best to soak the raw cashews overnight for this creamy vegan queso, but if you're short on time, follow the Ingredient tip for Cashew Cream (page 121).

2 cups raw cashews

½ cup unsweetened oat milk

¼ teaspoon sea salt

¼ cup nutritional yeast

Juice of 1 lemon

1 teaspoon ground turmeric

½ teaspoon garlic powder

½ teaspoon onion powder

¼ teaspoon chipotle powder (optional)

1. Put the cashews in a medium bowl and cover with cold water. Cover the bowl and soak overnight.

2. Drain the soaked cashews and add to a food processor or high-powered blender along with the oat milk, salt, nutritional yeast, lemon juice, turmeric, garlic powder, onion powder, and chipotle powder (if using). Blend until smooth.

3. To serve the queso warm, pour it into a small saucepan and heat through, stirring frequently.

VARIATION: *Any vegan milk alternative can also be used in place of oat milk.*

PER SERVING (2 TABLESPOONS): Calories: 101; Protein: 3g; Carbohydrates: 6g; Fiber: 1g; Total fat: 8g; Saturated fat: 1g; Sugar: 1g; Sodium: 25mg

PUMPKIN SEED PESTO

MAKES 3 cups   **PREP TIME** 15 minutes

Pumpkin seeds are a great source of protein, healthy fats, iron, magnesium, zinc, and important B vitamins. Make a batch of this pesto to add to dishes throughout the week.

4 garlic cloves, peeled

2 cups pumpkin seeds

**5 tablespoons
nutritional yeast**

½ teaspoon sea salt

¼ cup water

2 cups fresh basil leaves

¼ cup fresh lemon juice

¼ cup extra-virgin olive oil

In a food processor or a high-powered blender, combine the garlic, pumpkin seeds, nutritional yeast, salt, and water and process until smooth. With the machine running, add the basil, lemon juice, and olive oil and mix until smooth. Transfer to an airtight container and store in the refrigerator for up to 5 days or in the freezer for up to 3 months.

LEFTOVERS TIP: *A convenient way to store leftover pesto is to spoon it into an ice cube tray and freeze. A typical ice cube tray compartment holds 2 tablespoons. Once frozen, pop out the cubes and place in a resealable plastic bag. Simply add frozen pesto cubes to dishes while they're cooking, or thaw overnight in the refrigerator to use in spreads.*

PER SERVING (2 TABLESPOONS): Calories: 78; Protein: 3g; Carbohydrates: 2g; Fiber: 1g; Total fat: 7g; Saturated fat: 1g; Sugar: 0g; Sodium: 26mg

ROASTED GARLIC AND WHITE BEAN SPREAD

MAKES 2 cups   **PREP TIME** 10 minutes   **COOK TIME** 35 minutes

Roasting garlic sweetens it, creating a creamy, smoky, and mild-tasting spread. Mixed with pureed white beans, olive oil, and lemon, you have a spread that can be enjoyed with crudités or as a topping for bowls and salads.

1 head garlic

3½ tablespoons extra-virgin olive oil, divided

1 (15-ounce) can low-sodium cannellini beans, drained and rinsed

Juice of 1 lemon

½ teaspoon sea salt

⅛ teaspoon freshly ground black pepper

1 teaspoon paprika

1. Preheat the oven to 400°F.

2. Peel off the outer layers of the garlic head while leaving the head intact. With a knife, cut ¼ inch off the top of the garlic head to expose the cloves. Place on a 12-by-12-inch piece of aluminum foil and drizzle with ½ tablespoon of olive oil. Roast for 35 minutes, or until the garlic is soft and golden brown. Allow to cool.

3. Carefully squeeze the roasted garlic into a food processor and add the beans, lemon juice, salt, pepper, and remaining 3 tablespoons of olive oil. Puree until smooth.

4. Serve in a bowl, garnished with the paprika. Store leftovers in an airtight container in the refrigerator for up to 5 days.

VARIATION: *Any white bean, such as great northern or navy, will work in this recipe.*

PER SERVING (2 TABLESPOONS): Calories: 50; Protein: 2g; Carbohydrates: 4g; Fiber: 1g; Total fat: 3g; Saturated fat: 0g; Sugar: 0g; Sodium: 37mg

LEMON-CUMIN YOGURT SAUCE

MAKES 2 cups   **PREP TIME** 5 minutes

This is a go-to sauce to top any kind of roasted vegetables. The tartness of the lemon and Greek yogurt goes perfectly with the warm, sweet, earthy taste of the cumin. Add this tangy sauce to your favorite bowls and salads, too.

2 cups 2% plain
  Greek yogurt

1½ teaspoons
  ground cumin

2 garlic cloves, minced

½ teaspoon finely grated
  lemon zest

Juice of 1 lemon

¼ teaspoon sea salt

⅛ teaspoon freshly ground
  black pepper

In a medium bowl, mix together the yogurt, cumin, garlic, lemon zest, lemon juice, salt, and pepper. Store in an airtight container in the refrigerator for up to 5 days.

VARIATION: *To make this sauce vegan, simply swap out the Greek yogurt for a plant-based yogurt. Read the label carefully to avoid added sugar.*

PER SERVING (2 TABLESPOONS): Calories: 21; Protein: 1g; Carbohydrates: 2g; Fiber: 0g; Total fat: 1g; Saturated fat: 1g; Sugar: 2g; Sodium: 24mg

ROASTED RED PEPPER AND WALNUT SAUCE

MAKES 2 cups   **PREP TIME** 5 minutes

Walnuts are a nutrient-dense food that provides an excellent source of anti-oxidants, omega-3 fatty acids, polyphenols, and vitamin E. The rich nutrient profile of walnuts, along with their savory taste and buttery consistency, makes them a very versatile nut to incorporate into dishes. This sauce is a great topping for sandwiches and burgers.

1½ cups chopped walnuts

2 teaspoons paprika

1 teaspoon honey

¼ teaspoon sea salt

1 (12-ounce) jar roasted red peppers, drained

2 garlic cloves, minced

2 tablespoons extra-virgin olive oil

Juice of 1 lemon

In a food processor, pulse the walnuts to a crumble. Add the paprika, honey, salt, roasted peppers, garlic, olive oil, and lemon juice and blend until smooth. Transfer to an airtight container and store in the refrigerator for up to 5 days.

LEFTOVERS TIP: *Use leftovers for topping the Spinach and Potato Frittata (page 43) or Mushroom Breakfast Quesadillas (page 44).*

PER SERVING (2 TABLESPOONS): Calories: 96; Protein: 2g; Carbohydrates: 4g; Fiber: 1g; Total fat: 9g; Saturated fat: 1g; Sugar: 2g; Sodium: 61mg

GREEN TAHINI SAUCE

30

DF

GF

NF

OP

SF

MAKES 1½ cups   **PREP TIME** 5 minutes

Making your own sauces and dressings is easy, quick, and a sure way to eliminate excess salt, added sugar, unhealthy oils, and preservatives. I make a sauce early in the week and use it on dishes all week long. This green sauce with fresh herbs and spinach adds delicious flavor to a variety of salads, veggies, and other dishes.

½ cup chopped
  fresh cilantro

½ cup chopped
  fresh parsley

½ cup baby spinach

½ cup tahini

2 garlic cloves, peeled

¼ cup extra-virgin olive oil

Juice of 2 limes

½ teaspoon sea salt

3 tablespoons honey

In a food processor, combine the cilantro, parsley, spinach, tahini, garlic, olive oil, lime juice, salt, and honey and blend until smooth. Transfer to an airtight container and store in the refrigerator for up to 5 days.

VARIATION: *Not a fan of cilantro? Add an additional ½ cup parsley instead.*

PER SERVING (2 TABLESPOONS): Calories: 119; Protein: 2g; Carbohydrates: 7g; Fiber: 1g; Total fat: 10g; Saturated fat: 1g; Sugar: 5g; Sodium: 63mg

MAPLE-MUSTARD DIPPING SAUCE

MAKES 2 cups   **PREP TIME** 5 minutes

This tangy sauce is extremely versatile—the sweet and savory flavor combination pairs well with any vegetable. It's the perfect dipping sauce for Sweet Potato Cakes (page 52) or spread for paninis, sandwiches, or simple roasted vegetables.

1 cup 2% plain
  Greek yogurt

¼ cup pure maple syrup

¼ cup Dijon mustard

3 tablespoons extra-virgin
  olive oil

2 tablespoons apple
  cider vinegar

½ teaspoon sea salt

In a medium bowl, whisk together the yogurt, maple syrup, mustard, olive oil, vinegar, and salt. Store in an airtight container in the refrigerator for up to 5 days.

VARIATION: *If the tangy taste of Greek yogurt is not your favorite, replace it with skyr (also sold in the yogurt section of the dairy aisle). Skyr is an Icelandic dairy product that has a thick, creamy flavor without the tangy taste.*

PER SERVING (¼ CUP): Calories: 94; Protein: 1g; Carbohydrates: 9g; Fiber: 0g; Total fat: 6g; Saturated fat: 1g; Sugar: 7g; Sodium: 174mg

AVOCADO CREMA

MAKES 2½ cups   **PREP TIME** 5 minutes

I enjoy eating bowl meals during the week, and this creamy, nutrient-dense sauce tops many of them. If you are a cilantro fan, this dressing will soon become your favorite. If you are not, parsley can easily be used instead.

3 avocados, peeled
  and pitted

3 tablespoons chopped
  fresh cilantro

½ cup 2% Greek
  plain yogurt

2 tablespoons extra-virgin
  olive oil

Juice of 1 lime

1 teaspoon garlic powder

¼ teaspoon sea salt

Scoop the avocado flesh into a food processor. Add the cilantro, yogurt, olive oil, lime juice, garlic powder, and salt and blend until smooth. Transfer to an airtight container and store in the refrigerator for up to 5 days.

VARIATION: *The Greek yogurt adds extra creaminess but can easily be left out to make this sauce vegan.*

PER SERVING (¼ CUP): Calories: 130; Protein: 2g; Carbohydrates: 6g; Fiber: 4g; Total fat: 12g; Saturated fat: 2g; Sugar: 1g; Sodium: 41mg

HONEY BALSAMIC DRESSING

MAKES 1½ cups   **PREP TIME** 5 minutes

This dressing is easy and quick, and I always have the ingredients on hand in my kitchen. I often make it for guests because I know everyone will enjoy it. This simple olive oil and balsamic vinegar dressing with a hint of sweetness pairs well with all salad ingredients.

½ cup balsamic vinegar

2 garlic cloves, peeled

½ teaspoon sea salt

⅛ teaspoon freshly ground black pepper

¼ cup honey

3 tablespoons Dijon mustard

½ cup extra-virgin olive oil

In a food processor or high-powered blender, combine the vinegar, garlic, salt, black pepper, honey, and mustard. With the machine running, stream in the olive oil and continue to blend until smooth. Transfer to a jar and store in the refrigerator for up to 1 week.

INGREDIENT TIP: *Look for local honey when you go shopping. Farmers' markets often have it. Local honey contains a blend of the local pollens, which may reduce pollen allergy symptoms.*

PER SERVING (2 TABLESPOONS): Calories: 113; Protein: 0g; Carbohydrates: 8g; Fiber: 0g; Total fat: 9g; Saturated fat: 1g; Sugar: 7g; Sodium: 94mg

CARROT-GINGER DRESSING

MAKES 2 cups   **PREP TIME** 5 minutes

This dressing is an easy and versatile one to always have in the refrigerator. Use it as a dip for Sweet Potato Cakes (page 52) or to top the Mango-Ginger Rice Bowls (page 72) or Beet Poke Bowls (page 73).

6 large carrots, peeled and chopped

2 tablespoons chopped fresh ginger

½ cup extra-virgin olive oil

½ cup unseasoned rice vinegar

3 tablespoons honey

1 tablespoon sesame oil

3 tablespoons 50% reduced-sodium tamari

In a food processor, combine the carrots and pulse until finely ground. Add the ginger, olive oil, vinegar, honey, sesame oil, and tamari and blend until smooth. Transfer to an airtight container and store in the refrigerator for up to 5 days.

INGREDIENT TIP: *Tamari is a Japanese soy sauce made from fermented soybeans. Typically, tamari is processed without wheat, making it a gluten-free alternative to soy sauce.*

PER SERVING (2 TABLESPOONS): Calories: 94; Protein: 1g; Carbohydrates: 6g; Fiber: 1g; Total fat: 8g; Saturated fat: 1g; Sugar: 5g; Sodium: 115mg

CHIPOTLE TAHINI DRESSING

MAKES 1½ cups   **PREP TIME** 15 minutes

This creamy, spicy dressing is perfect for topping omelets, salads, tacos, and sandwiches. The nutty taste of the tahini, paired with the smoky spiciness of the chipotle peppers, creates a delicious finish to a wide variety of dishes.

¼ cup tahini

½ cup 2% plain
  Greek yogurt

¼ cup apple cider vinegar

Juice of 1 lime

1 tablespoon honey

2 canned chipotles in
  adobo sauce

1 teaspoon garlic powder

½ teaspoon sea salt

In a food processor, combine the tahini, yogurt, vinegar, lime juice, honey, chipotles, garlic powder, and salt and blend until smooth. Transfer to an airtight container and store in the refrigerator for up to 5 days.

VARIATION: *Replace the honey with agave nectar and the Greek yogurt with dairy-free yogurt for a vegan alternative.*

PER SERVING (2 TABLESPOONS): Calories: 44; Protein: 1g; Carbohydrates: 4g; Fiber: 1g; Total fat: 3g; Saturated fat: 1g; Sugar: 2g; Sodium: 59mg

MEASUREMENT CONVERSIONS

	US STANDARD	US STANDARD (ounces)	METRIC (approximate)
VOLUME EQUIVALENTS *(Liquid)*	2 tablespoons	1 fl. oz.	30 mL
	¼ cup	2 fl. oz.	60 mL
	½ cup	4 fl. oz.	120 mL
	1 cup	8 fl. oz.	240 mL
	1½ cups	12 fl. oz.	355 mL
	2 cups or 1 pint	16 fl. oz.	475 mL
	4 cups or 1 quart	32 fl. oz.	1 L
	1 gallon	128 fl. oz.	4 L
VOLUME EQUIVALENTS *(Dry)*	⅛ teaspoon	————	0.5 mL
	¼ teaspoon	————	1 mL
	½ teaspoon	————	2 mL
	¾ teaspoon	————	4 mL
	1 teaspoon	————	5 mL
	1 tablespoon	————	15 mL
	¼ cup	————	59 mL
	⅓ cup	————	79 mL
	½ cup	————	118 mL
	⅔ cup	————	156 mL
	¾ cup	————	177 mL
	1 cup	————	235 mL
	2 cups or 1 pint	————	475 mL
	3 cups	————	700 mL
	4 cups or 1 quart	————	1 L
WEIGHT EQUIVALENTS	½ ounce	————	15 g
	1 ounce	————	30 g
	2 ounces	————	60 g
	4 ounces	————	115 g
	8 ounces	————	225 g
	12 ounces	————	340 g
	16 ounces or 1 pound	————	455 g

	FAHRENHEIT	CELSIUS (approximate)
OVEN TEMPERATURES	250°F	120°C
	300°F	150°C
	325°F	180°C
	375°F	190°C
	400°F	200°C
	425°F	220°C
	450°F	230°C

RESOURCES

Environmental Working Group

EWG.org/foodnews

This nonprofit, nonpartisan organization is dedicated to helping consumers make safer and more informed decisions about the products they buy. The food news section of their website provides up-to-date information on how to reduce your exposure to pesticides in produce.

Produce for Better Health Foundation

FruitsAndVeggies.org

The Produce for Better Health Foundation shares many tools to help consumers enjoy more fruits and vegetables every day. You'll find recipes, advice from experts, and nutrition and storing information.

Seasonal Food Guide

SeasonalFoodGuide.org

The Seasonal Food Guide helps consumers select locally grown produce that is in peak season at any time, any place.

The Vegetarian Resource Group

VRG.org

This site is run by a nonprofit organization dedicated to educating consumers on how to eat well with a vegetarian lifestyle. Find health information, recipes, guides, and handouts on their website.

REFERENCES

Carr, A. C., and S. Maggini. "Vitamin C and Immune Function." *Nutrients* 9, no. 11 (November 2017): 1211. doi:10.3390/nu9111211

Farvid, M. S., W. Y. Chen, B. A. Rosner, R. M. Tamimi, W. C. Willett, and A. H. Eliassen. "Fruit and Vegetable Consumption and Breast Cancer Incidence: Repeated Measures Over 30 Years of Follow-up." *International Journal of Cancer* 144, no. 7 (July 2018): 1496–1510. doi:10.1002/ijc.31653

Huang, Z., Y. Liu, G. Qi, D. Brand, and S. G. Zheng. "Role of Vitamin A in the Immune System." *Journal of Clinical Medicine* 7, no. 9 (September 2018): 258. doi:10.3390/jcm7090258

Rico-Campà, A., M. A. Martínez-González, I. Alvarez-Alvarez, R. D. Mendonça, C. de la Fuente-Arrillaga, C. Gómez-Donoso, and M. Bes-Rastrollo. "Association between Consumption of Ultra-processed Foods and All Cause Mortality: SUN Prospective Cohort Study." *BMJ* 365 (May 2019): l949. doi:10.1136/bmj.l1949

Srour B., L. K. Fezeu, E. Kesse-Guyot, B. Allès, C. Méjean, R. M. Andrianasolo et al. 2019. "Ultra-Processed Food Intake and Risk of Cardiovascular Disease: Prospective Cohort Study (NutriNet-Santé)." *British Medical Journal* 365:l1451. doi:10.1136/bmj.l1451

St.-Onge, M. P., A. Roberts, A. Shechter, A. R. Choudhury. "Fiber and Saturated Fat Are Associated with Sleep Arousals and Slow Wave Sleep." *Journal of Clinical Sleep Medicine* 12, no. 1 (January 2016): 19–24. doi:10.5664/jcsm.5384

US Department of Agriculture and US Department of Health and Human Services. *Dietary Guidelines for Americans, 2020–2025*. 9th Edition. December 2020. DietaryGuidelines.gov

Weaver, C. M., J. Dwyer, V. L. Fulgoni III, J. C. King, G. A. Leveille, R. S. MacDonald, J. Ordovas, and D. Schnakenberg. "Processed Foods: Contributions to Nutrition." *American Journal of Clinical Nutrition* 99, no. 6 (April 2014): 1525–1542. doi:10.3945/ajcn.114.089284

Wintergerst, E. S., S. Maggini, and D. H. Hornig. "Immune-enhancing Role of Vitamin C and Zinc and Effect on Clinical Conditions." *Annals of Nutrition and Metabolism* 50, no. 2 (February 2006): 85–94. doi:10.1159/000090495

INDEX

H

I

ACKNOWLEDGMENTS

I am forever grateful for my husband, David, who supports my never-ending projects and always encourages me to follow my passion. To my children, Alex and Annabelle, thank you for your brutally honest taste-testing feedback. You two drive me every day to keep creating healthy, delicious food. I am so proud to see you both growing up to enjoy cooking as much as I do.

A huge thank you to my talented editor, Kelly Koester, for her guidance, positive feedback, and encouragement, as well as to the entire Callisto Media editing team. It was a pleasure to work with all of you. Finally, many thanks to Callisto Media for making this book possible, and to Katie Parr for bringing me another great opportunity.

ABOUT THE AUTHOR

Kathy Siegel, MS, RDN, CDN, is a nationally renowned food and nutrition expert, with a Master of Science degree in health communication from Boston University. Kathy has more than two decades of expertise as a registered dietitian nutritionist (RDN) working in wellness, integrative nutrition, culinary nutrition, and health marketing communication. Kathy is the author of *The 30-Minute Clean Eating Cookbook* (Rockridge Press) and founder of Kathy Siegel Nutrition, where she works with health food brands and commodity boards. Kathy is also a contributing writer and media spokesperson. Her expertise has been included in publications and media including NBC News, Food Network, *U.S. News & World Report*, Livestrong, *The Independent*, and *Reader's Digest*.

CPSIA information can be obtained
at www.ICGtesting.com
Printed in the USA
JSHW010913290521
15361JS00005B/39